Table of contents

OECD ECONOMIC SURVEYS: INDONESIA: ECONOMIC ASSESMENT – ISBN 978-92-64-04805-8 – © OECD 2008

This Economic Assessment was prepared in the Economics Department by Luiz de Mello and Diego Moccero, under the supervision of Peter Jarrett.

Consultancy support was provided by Margherita Comola, Hal Hill and Arianto Patunru.

Research assistance was provided by Anne Legendre and secretarial assistance by Mee-Lan Frank.

The Economic Assessment was discussed at a meeting of the Economic and Development Review Committee on 9 June 2008.

This book has...

StatLinks

A service that delivers Excel® files
from the printed page!

Look for the *StatLinks* at the bottom right-hand corner of the tables or graphs in this book. To download the matching Excel® spreadsheet, just type the link into your Internet browser, starting with the *http://dx.doi.org* prefix.
If you're reading the PDF e-book edition, and your PC is connected to the Internet, simply click on the link. You'll find *StatLinks* appearing in more OECD books.

BASIC STATISTICS OF INDONESIA (2007 unless noted)

THE LAND

Area (thousands sq. km)	1 919
Total area (thousands sq. km, territorial and EEZ)	5 800

POPULATION

Total (millions)	224.9
Inhabitants per sq. km	117.2
Net average annual increase during 2000-06 (in per cent)	1.3
Urbanisation rate (2006, in per cent)	49.0
Age distribution (2004, in % of total population)	
0-14	28.2
15-64	66.4
65+	4.9

EMPLOYMENT

Working-age population (2006, in millions)	160.8
Total employment (2006, in millions)	95.5
Average annual labour force growth during 2000-06 (in per cent)	1.9
Labour force participation rate (2006, in per cent)	66.2
Unemployment rate (2006, BPS definition, in per cent)	10.3
Informality rate (*Economic Assessment* definition, in per cent, 2004)	69.6

GROSS DOMESTIC PRODUCT

GDP at current prices and current exchange rate (USD billion)	432.8
Per capita GDP at current prices and market exchange rate (USD)	1 924.6
Average annual real growth over previous 5 years (in %)	5.5
Gross fixed capital formation (GFCF) in % of GDP	24.9

PUBLIC FINANCES (% of GDP)

Revenue	17.9
Primary balance	19.1
Nominal balance	−1.2
Gross debt	35.0

INDICATORS OF LIVING STANDARDS

Doctors per 1 000 inhabitants (2003)	0.13
Infant mortality per 1 000 live births (2005)	36.0
Life expectancy at birth (2005)	68.1
Human Development Index (2005)	69.6
Upper-secondary educational attainment (2006)	20.1
Literacy rate (2006, in per cent of 15+ population)	90.0
Income inequality (2005, Gini coefficient)	0.36
Poverty incidence (2006, national poverty line)	17.8
Internet users per 1 000 inhabitants (2005)	72.5

FOREIGN TRADE

Exports of goods (USD billion)	118.0
In % of GDP	26.9
Average annual growth over previous 5 years (%)	14.9
Imports of goods (USD billion)	85.3
In % of GDP	19.5
Average annual growth over previous 5 years (%)	19.6

Executive summary

Growth is picking up, helping to close a still sizeable gap in living standards relative to the OECD area

Indonesia's economic performance has improved markedly over the last few years. The economy has recovered in earnest from the 1997-98 financial crisis, and GDP growth has been around 5½ per cent per year since 2004. This rate is below that of some regional peers, but high enough to deliver broad-based improvements in living standards. The contribution of private consumption has trended up, especially since 2004, on the back of robust credit creation. Investment also appears to be rebounding, although it remains lower than elsewhere in the region when measured in relation to GDP. Export growth has been supported by high commodity prices. The momentum of the current expansion is expected to be maintained in 2008-09, with GDP growth likely exceeding 6% per year. Yet, the current level of growth is insufficient to speed up the pace of reduction in poverty and unemployment. Therefore, raising the economy's growth potential and sustaining it over the longer term is Indonesia's foremost policy challenge. To achieve this, concerted efforts are required in several areas, especially if the goals set out in *Vision 2030* – a well thought-out initiative by a group of independent experts to achieve high growth – are to be fulfilled. Against this background, this *Economic Assessment* discusses a number of policy options for improving the business climate and making better use of labour inputs. Progress in these areas will contribute to enhancing economic efficiency further, so as to narrow the gap in relative living standards that currently exists between Indonesia and the more prosperous countries in the OECD area.

Fiscal performance is improving and should remain strong

Responsible conduct of fiscal policy in an increasingly decentralised setting has delivered low budget deficits and falling public indebtedness in relation to GDP. The budget has therefore benefitted from an "interest dividend", which has allowed the authorities to begin to reallocate scarce resources towards meritorious programmes in the social and infrastructure development areas. Emphasis on human capital accumulation, and particularly on improvements in the quality of services, including labour training, would be particularly welcome, given that Indonesia's educational attainment indicators fare particularly poorly in relation to some regional comparator countries and the OECD area. Efforts are also under way to strengthen tax administration, to alleviate the income tax burden on the business sector and to improve value-added taxation. Decentralisation, which has put the local governments at the helm of service delivery since 2001, was implemented rapidly and yet without disruption. There is broad agreement that, based on its favourable public debt dynamics, Indonesia will in all likelihood continue to benefit from a relatively comfortable fiscal position in the years to come. Therefore, the time is now ripe for building on past achievements, which are commendable, and for strengthening the fiscal framework further.

There is room for further reducing price subsidies
for fuel and electricity

Indonesia continues to subsidise fuel and electricity consumption by maintaining a sizeable gap between domestic and international oil prices. Subsidies are expected to make up about 20% of central government expenditure in 2008, with those on fuel taking up the lion's share of the total. A few selected food items are also subsidised, but such outlays account for a small share of outlays on subsidies. Efforts to eliminate fuel price subsidisation have yielded mixed results. For example, a mechanism introduced in 2001-02 for automatically adjusting domestic prices so as to reduce the gap between domestic and international fuel prices was abolished not long after. These subsidies are an inefficient use of scarce budgetary resources at a time when resources are needed for human capital accumulation and infrastructure development, in addition to creating considerable fiscal stress when international fuel prices are high. First and foremost, a significant share of government spending on some subsidies (about two-thirds in the case of fuel, according to official estimates) accrue to individuals in the top two quintiles of the income distribution, rather than benefitting vulnerable social groups. These subsidies also make it difficult for the oil and electricity companies to pursue their commercial objectives independently of the government's social policies. Moreover, extensive subsidisation complicates the regulatory framework, because uncertainty in price setting discourages much needed private investment in these sectors. Finally, by keeping the price of fossil fuels artificially low, such price support encourages wasteful consumption and discourages a search for alternative sources of energy, with a detrimental impact on the environment. Therefore, the authorities' efforts to gradually reduce the gap between domestic and international energy prices would be welcome, provided that targeted compensatory measures (discussed below) are taken to shield the needy from the attendant price rises. The increase in domestic fuel prices by nearly 30% in mid-May was a step in the right direction, but the introduction of a formula-based mechanism for setting domestic fuel prices would have the advantage of making price changes transparent and removing them from the political arena.

The monetary policy regime can be strengthened
further

Monetary policy has been conducted within a fully-fledged inflation-targeting regime since mid-2005, when monetary targeting was formally abandoned. Following an upsurge in 2005-06 as a result of fuel-price hikes, inflation was reduced and kept within the end-year target range of 5-7% in 2007. Increases in food and energy prices are nevertheless weighing on inflation outcomes yet again. Headline inflation and expectations have risen and are now well above the ceiling of the target range of 4-6% for 2008. The effect of high food prices on inflation is particularly strong in emerging-market economies, where these items account for a comparatively high proportion of the consumer-price index. To strengthen credibility in the policy regime, the central bank is advised to react pre-emptively by tightening the monetary policy stance should the outlook for inflation and expectations deteriorate further. International experience shows that resolute, forward-looking action is essential for anchoring expectations and enhancing policy credibility in countries that have a short track record with inflation targeting. Over the longer term, policy effort should also focus on lowering inflation towards the average of Indonesia's main trading partners. The announcement of gradually decreasing targets for the coming years, from 4-6% in 2008 to 3-5% over the medium term, is therefore a welcome signal of commitment to inflation convergence, which will require a sustained effort to achieve those targets.

The financial sector has recovered in earnest from the crisis

The steps taken to strengthen the financial sector since the financial crisis of 1997-98, including the most recent biennial Structural Reform Programme, have largely paid off: the banking system is sound, capital-adequacy and liquidity indicators have improved over the years, and the quality of loan portfolios has been strengthened. Nevertheless, State-owned banks have a large presence in the sector, in part due to the rescue of failing banks after the crisis, and the non-bank sector is relatively small. Credit-to-GDP ratios are lower than in regional peers and Indonesia's pre-crisis level, despite a robust expansion over the last few years. As in other countries with a large informal sector, access to credit is particularly difficult for small and unregistered enterprises, which tend to rely on informal, costly sources of finance. Indonesia would therefore benefit from further financial deepening, including in particular the development of the non-bank market segment and an expansion of credit to small businesses. Progress in this area could unleash opportunities for entrepreneurship, but policy action should continue to be guided by high standards of financial-sector supervision and prudential regulations.

There is plenty of room for making product-market regulations more pro-competition

Pro-competition product-market regulations tend to be growth-enhancing, because the reallocation of inputs towards higher-productivity sectors is unencumbered. An assessment of Indonesia's regulatory environment on the basis of the OECD methodology for gauging competitive pressures in product markets suggests considerable scope for improvement. In particular, despite recent deregulation efforts and reforms, Indonesia still fares particularly poorly in comparison with OECD countries in terms of the size and scope of government. For example, the government owns all or the majority of large firms in several sectors, including network industries. It is also involved in manufacturing and services, including banking and insurance. Sector-specific restrictions on private-sector involvement also remain, including in transport and retail distribution, as well as foreign ownership ceilings, as discussed below. Options are being put forward by the authorities for liberalising State-owned monopolies in key network industries, which would contribute to opening up opportunities for the private sector. The experience of several countries in the OECD area and beyond suggests that, with appropriately designed regulatory frameworks, the withdrawal of the State from network industries has been accompanied by an expansion of supply and a reduction in service prices, as well as increases in productivity.

Sustaining high growth calls for improvements in the business climate

There is near-consensual agreement that long-term growth is being held back more by supply- rather than demand-side constraints. The private sector can play a prominent role in the growth process, so long as the business climate can be improved considerably. Economic and regulatory uncertainty, deficiencies in law enforcement and infrastructure bottlenecks are among the main barriers to entrepreneurship. Indonesia's ranking in international indicators of perceived corruption also suggests that there is significant room for improvement in that area too. The authorities are aware of the need to take decisive action to tackle these deficiencies, and there has been unequivocal progress in some policy domains in recent years. In particular, enactment of the Investment Law in 2007 was a considerable step forward. The Law makes the investment regime more transparent to investors, and ensures equal treatment for domestic and foreign investment. Screening, notification and approval procedures have been simplified, but ownership ceilings remain in many sectors. As a result, Indonesia's FDI legislation remains more restrictive than those of most OECD countries on the basis of the OECD methodology for assessing and comparing FDI regimes across countries. Further liberalisation of foreign ownership restrictions could therefore be envisaged in support of policy efforts to encourage investment and boost entrepreneurship. Policy effort in this area would therefore be welcome to nurture investor confidence in the new FDI regime.

More can be done to encourage much needed investment

Indonesia's ratio of investment to GDP remains below those of regional comparator countries. This has raised concern among policymakers about the country's ability to lift and maintain potential growth over the longer term and to match the growth rates of the fastest-growing economies in the region, including China and India. At the same time, Indonesia has some of the weakest infrastructure development indicators in Southeast Asia, suggesting ample pent-up demand for such investment. A strong fiscal position is creating room in the budget for increasing government spending on infrastructure. But greater private-sector involvement in infrastructure development and maintenance would be essential. For that, regulatory uncertainty must be reduced, especially with reference to the pricing of water/sanitation services, fuels and electricity. Price subsidisation complicates investment decisions, because it makes it difficult for investors to assess the rates of return of projects. Existing restrictions on foreign ownership in these sectors also constrains private-sector involvement. The design of a new, pro-investment regulatory framework, including price liberalisation, free entry into network industries and the setting up of independent regulators would obviously be a complex task but could create attractive opportunities for the private sector to participate in infrastructure development.

Business regulations by local governments
are onerous to the private sector and need
to be reduced

The decentralisation programme that was implemented in 2001 granted local governments considerable autonomy to issue business regulations, including licenses, and to levy fees and user charges for the provision of local services. Based on this prerogative, most jurisdictions have introduced several levies, often without the accord of the central government, as a means of raising revenue. Central government efforts to tackle this problem have so far yielded mixed results. Initiatives have nevertheless been put in place, including by independent think-tanks, to raise awareness among district-level policymakers of the undesirable effects of a proliferation of local regulations on business activity. These efforts seem to be bearing fruit. Several local governments are setting up one-stop shops as a means of facilitating business registration and the issuance of licenses. Also, legislation is under consideration by the central government to abolish local levies that are deemed in breach of nation-wide regulations. Continued efforts to simplify business regulation procedures further and to make them more business-friendly would therefore be welcome. Steadfast progress in this area is crucial for rendering the regulatory framework more transparent and pro-investment.

Capacity bottlenecks at the local level will
need to be removed to ensure a recovery
in public investment

Decentralisation has put the local governments at the forefront of service delivery, including in public investment programmes. But capacity constraints have resulted in a backlog of investment projects. At the same time, delays in approval of local government budgets by the Ministry of Home Affairs, which is required by law, have taken a toll on the implementation of investment projects. In addition, a focus on short-term, calendar-year budgeting makes it difficult for local governments to carry out and finance multi-year investment projects. Anecdotal evidence suggests that deficiencies in public procurement and tighter oversight in the context of the authorities' ongoing anti-corruption initiatives have made local government officials wary of executing budgetary commitments for fear of prosecution. This may be an unavoidable short-term cost of anti-corruption efforts towards boosting accountability at the all levels of government over time. The stock of unspent budgetary appropriations, especially those financed through revenue sharing with the natural resource-rich jurisdictions, has increased over time, taking a toll on the government's ability to implement investment projects. There is, therefore, considerable scope for reducing capacity constraints at the local level and for making budgetary processes, including central government approval of local government budgets, swifter and better equipped to deal with the multi-year nature of investment projects.

Greater flexibility in employment protection
legislation would make for a better use
of labour inputs

Better utilisation of labour inputs is another pre-requisite for putting growth on a higher, sustainable trajectory. A tightening of labour legislation, especially with enactment of the Manpower Law of 2003, has contributed to poor labour-market outcomes. These include high unemployment, persistent informality and a loss of dynamism in labour-intensive manufacturing sectors, such as textiles, clothing and footwear, in which Indonesia has a comparative advantage. Indonesia's labour legislation is rigid in relation to most countries in the OECD area, and particularly in comparison with regional peers. On the basis of the OECD methodology for assessing the stringency of a country's employment protection legislation (EPL), the Indonesian labour code is particularly restrictive on regular contracts, due essentially to bureaucratic dismissal procedures and costly severance-pay requirements. There are also constraints on the use of temporary and fixed-term contractual arrangements, because of strict provisions on the duration and number of extensions of such contracts, as well as on the nature of the activities and occupations to which such arrangements apply. Alternative indicators, such as those featured in the World Bank's *Doing Business* reports, also underscore the stringency of Indonesia's EPL in comparison with regional peers and OECD countries. Several options can be considered for making labour legislation more flexible. In particular, consideration could be given to simplifying procedures for dismissals in the case of regular contracts, relaxing restrictions on temporary work and fixed-term contracts, and reducing the burden of severance pay and long-term compensation on employers.

Minimum wage legislation should also be
reviewed

At about 65% of the median wage of salaried workers, the minimum wage is already relatively high in Indonesia in comparison with OECD countries. It has risen fast, especially after decentralisation in 2001, because the task of setting the value of the minimum wage is now under the local governments' purview. This increase has had a deleterious impact on labour-market performance: increases in the minimum wage that are out of step with productivity gains are likely to displace lower-skilled workers. As in the case of EPL stringency, the loss of dynamism in labour-intensive sectors can be attributed to a large extent to the rising relative value of the minimum wage. Therefore, further increases in the minimum wage could be capped so as not to exceed labour productivity gains. This, or, if it were possible, a gradual reduction over time would help to alleviate the adverse employment impact of such a high minimum wage (in relation to the median) on low-skilled workers and to facilitate formalisation in the labour market.

Enhanced social protection could complement
efforts to make the labour code more flexible

Burdensome labour laws, including minimum-wage provisions, often penalise vulnerable workers, instead of protecting them. This is because legal provisions are not binding in the informal sector, where income is likely to be lower and job security more precarious. Also, increases in the minimum wage are most harmful to the workers at greatest risk of job losses in the formal sector. Therefore, policy initiatives to build effective social protection while making the labour code more flexible could yield considerable dividends, including in terms of labour-market performance. To make tangible progress in this area, several policy options could be considered. For example, unemployment insurance could be introduced in lieu of onerous dismissal/severance compensation entitlements. There are several options for designing an effective unemployment insurance scheme. But, as a general rule, it is important that such schemes be fiscally sound and affordable to workers and employers. At the same time, budget finances permitting, formal social insurance programmes could be developed. To this end, once credibility in the existing social insurance programme (*Jamsostek*) has been built, participation could be extended to the self-employed and employees in smaller enterprises on a voluntary basis, as envisaged by the 2004 Social Security Law (*Jamsosnas*). Policy action in this area would be welcome to broaden the array of options for saving for retirement and to facilitate access to health care for those workers and their families who are currently uninsured. In any case, it should be acknowledged that the attractiveness of coverage, both by unemployment and social insurance, depends ultimately on the perceived benefits of social protection and the affordability of contributions, which may be a significant constraint for individuals on low incomes.

Social assistance programmes could be improved

Indonesia already has a number of formal, government-financed safety nets. The authorities' efforts to strengthen these programmes since the 1997-98 financial crisis through community-based and targeted income transfers to vulnerable and poor individuals are commendable. These programmes are perceived to be working well, following efforts to improve targeting and governance in the delivery of benefits. Emphasis is now shifting towards enhancing social assistance by equipping vulnerable individuals with the minimum skills needed to pull themselves out of poverty. This change is of course welcome. To build on previous achievements, conditionality could be improved in the main existing income transfer programme (*Program Keluarga Harapan*) to strengthen the link between social protection and durable improvements in social outcomes. International experience, especially in the Latin America countries that pioneered the design of conditional income transfers, suggests that the most effective eligibility requirements are related to school attendance and participation in preventive health care programmes. Complementary initiatives can also be taken to improve the targeting of overall government social spending. A reduction in outlays on price subsidies for fuels and electricity, which are on balance poorly targeted, as mentioned above, would be a starting point. Budgetary resources could then be diverted to the financing of programmes that do reach the most vulnerable segments of society, improving the overall progressivity of social spending.

Chapter 1

Growth performance and policy challenges

Indonesia's growth performance is improving, following a slow recovery from the 1997-98 financial crisis. Growth is becoming increasingly reliant on the dynamism of domestic demand, rather than net exports. Investment is picking up, despite considerable business-climate obstacles to entrepreneurship. Unemployment remains high, and labour informality is pervasive, due predominantly to an increasingly onerous labour code.

The macroeconomic policy setting is by and large appropriate. Fiscal policy has been conducted responsibly and in an increasingly decentralised manner. Public indebtedness has been reduced, creating room in the budget for raising spending on much needed infrastructure development, human capital accumulation and social protection. Monetary policy is now conducted within a fully-fledged inflation-targeting regime. It has delivered disinflation, albeit to a level of inflation that remains above that of Indonesia's trading partners. Efforts to enhance credibility in the monetary policy framework would be helpful.

This Economic Assessment argues that the main barriers to raising the economy's growth potential are to be found on the supply side of the economy. Indonesia will need to improve the business environment and make better use of labour inputs to put the economy on a higher growth trajectory. The country's income gap relative to the OECD is sizeable, and several years of sustained growth will be needed to eliminate it.

After a comparatively slow recovery from the 1997-98 financial crisis that affected several countries in Southeast Asia and beyond, Indonesia's growth performance has improved markedly in recent years. GDP grew by 6.3% in 2007, the fastest pace of expansion since the crisis. Net exports continue to perform well, but most of the increase in output growth in recent years has come from domestic sources. Nevertheless, unemployment remains stubbornly high, and informality is pervasive in the labour market. Fiscal policy continues to be conducted responsibly, delivering falling public indebtedness, and public services are provided in an increasingly decentralised manner. The institutional framework for the conduct of monetary policy was strengthened with the implementation of fully-fledged inflation targeting in mid-2005. Inflation came down in 2007, following an upsurge in 2005-06 on the heels of a significant reduction in fuel subsidies, but is now trending up again due to higher food and fuel prices.

For a country of Indonesia's income level, an important long-term policy challenge is to raise potential growth so as to secure a convergence in living standards with respect to the more prosperous countries in the OECD area. To achieve this, policy initiatives will be needed in several domains, as recognised in a document (*Visi Indonesia 2030*) published by a group of independent analysts, which lays out their long-term vision for Indonesia. They hope to raise the economy's potential growth rate to about 8.5% per year on average during 2006-30 to place Indonesia among the five largest economies in the world at the end of their planning horizon. This is important, because the current growth level is not high enough to lead to a sustained reduction in poverty and unemployment over the longer term.

This chapter discusses Indonesia's growth performance since the 1997-98 financial crisis and identifies the main policy challenges that will need to be addressed to raise the economy's growth potential in a sustainable manner. Attention is devoted to the main obstacles to entrepreneurship and effective utilisation of labour resources, which will be dealt with in greater detail in Chapters 2 and 3, respectively.

Recovery from the 1997-98 crisis

Indonesia has now fully recovered from the 1997-98 financial crisis. Nevertheless, international comparisons suggest that the country's post-crisis adjustment has been slower than in regional peers, where an upsurge in investment and exports sustained growth and job creation in the aftermath of the crisis (Figure 1.1). Indonesian GDP grew at about the average of comparator countries over the period leading up to the crisis, but slowed down considerably thereafter, despite a recovery in recent years. In particular:

● Investment was the component of demand that suffered the sharpest decline at the time of the crisis, a development that can be attributed to a large extent to a reversal in FDI inflows (discussed below). Gross fixed capital formation has bounced back since 2000, and has now approached its 1997 level in real terms, when the crisis erupted. By

Figure 1.1. **The Asian crisis and economic performance: Cross-country comparisons, 1990-2006**

1997 = 100

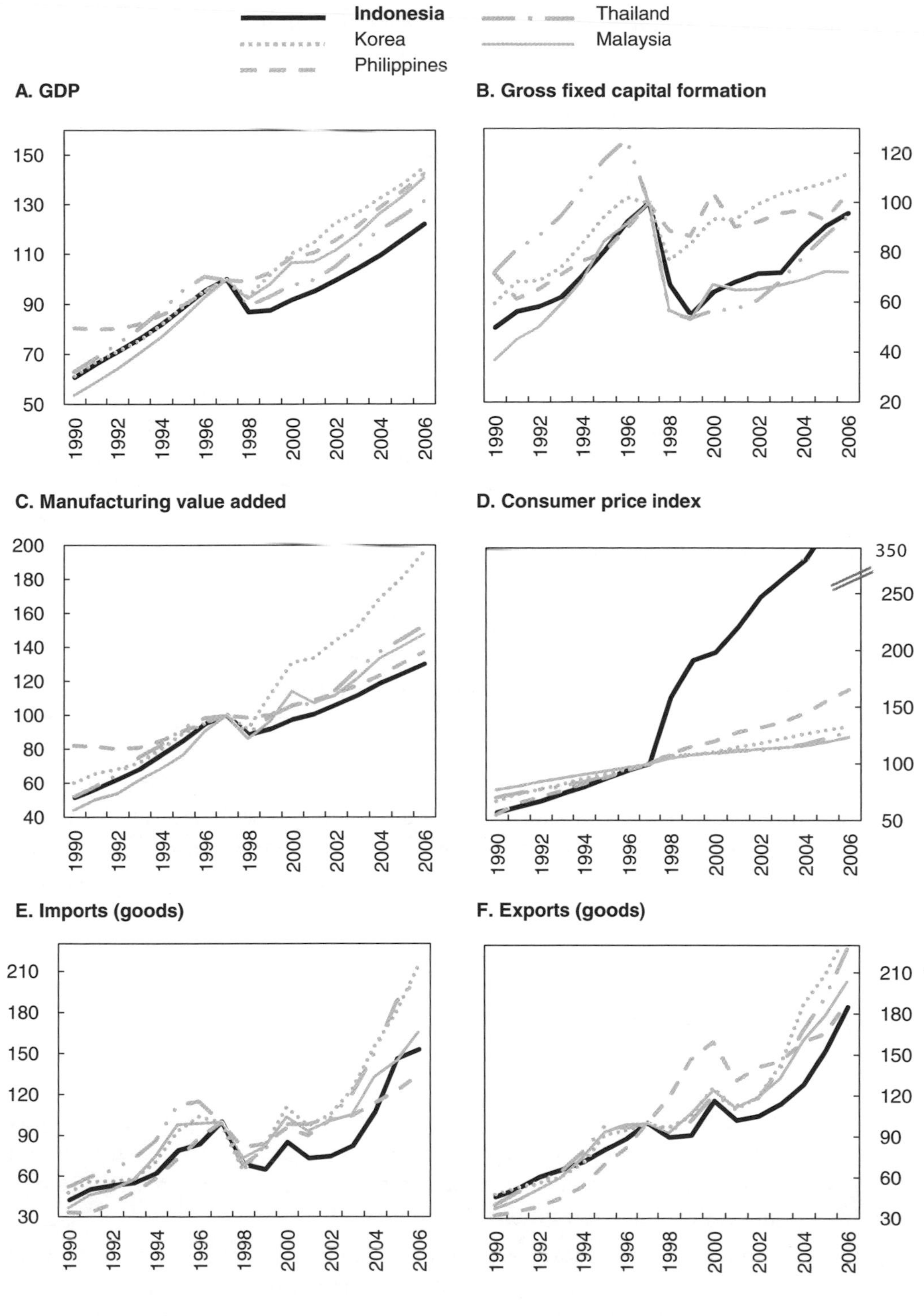

Indonesia   Thailand
Korea   Malaysia
Philippines

A. GDP

B. Gross fixed capital formation

C. Manufacturing value added

D. Consumer price index

E. Imports (goods)

F. Exports (goods)

StatLink 🔗 http://dx.doi.org/10.1787/414525406465

Source: World Bank (World Development Indicators) and OECD calculations.

contrast, the post-crisis recovery in investment was particularly swift in Korea and, to a milder extent, the Philippines.

- From the supply side, the turnaround in manufacturing value added has also been slower in Indonesia than in comparator countries, although it had recovered to its pre-crisis level by 2000. This lack of dynamism in manufacturing growth after the crisis poses challenges for the future. All sectors were affected by the crisis, although agriculture was comparatively more resilient.[1]

- Inflation has been higher in Indonesia since the crisis than in regional peers. This is due in part to the large nominal depreciation of the *rupiah* during the crisis. The Indonesian currency depreciated in nominal terms by far more than any other currency in the region. The ensuing rise in inflation, which reached about 80% on an annualised basis during the first half of 1998, eroded most of the initial boost to competitiveness arising from a weaker currency.

- Indonesia's export growth has been the lowest among the crisis-hit countries, especially in manufactured goods. The contraction in exports was the sharpest in the region in the wake of the crisis, although growth has picked up in recent years.[2] Most of the post-crisis expansion in exports has come from non-manufactured goods, including non-agricultural commodities, supported predominantly by price gains, rather than volume growth. The deceleration of volume growth after the crisis was particularly severe in the case of labour-intensive industries, including textiles and footwear.[3] By contrast, the rebound in trade flows was particularly pronounced in Korea, which explains to some extent that country's swift turnaround after the crisis.

Indonesia's larger fall during the crisis and its failure to recover as promptly as its neighbours suggests that important obstacles must have been at play. These include not only macroeconomic imbalances, reflected in higher inflation, but also a comparatively less supportive business environment, which has discouraged entrepreneurship and prevented a more effective use of labour inputs, with comparatively high unemployment and persistent segmentation in the labour market due to widespread informality (discussed in Chapter 3). This *Economic Assessment* argues that Indonesia will need to tackle these weaknesses to raise the economy's growth potential and to sustain it over the longer term.

What drives Indonesian growth?

Growth performance and relative income gap

Growth has slowed down since the crisis but appears to have regained dynamism since 2004. Real GDP grew on average by 8.1% per year during 1989-96 but decelerated to 5.1% on average during 2002-06 (Figure 1.2), a period that excludes the crisis years and the ensuing immediate recovery. From the demand side, the contribution of private consumption appears to be trending up, especially after 2004, following a few years of predominantly net export- and investment-driven growth.

From the supply side, manufacturing output expanded rapidly after liberalising reforms in the mid-1980s on the back of rising export demand. But it now appears to be losing momentum (Table 1.1), particularly in the sectors where Indonesia has a comparative advantage, including natural resources (particularly wood, oil and gas) and labour-intensive activities, such as the production of textiles, clothing and footwear. The electronics, including electrical appliances, and automotive industries have nevertheless

Figure 1.2. **Indonesia's long-term growth performance**
In per cent

A. GDP growth and contributions, 1985-2007

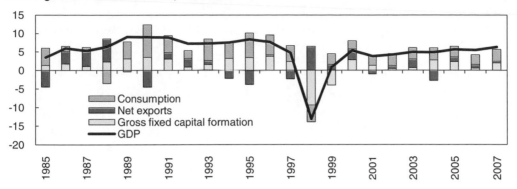

B. Structure of supply, 1985-2007

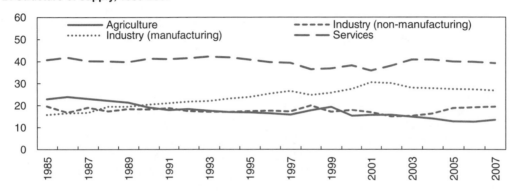

C. Relative income trends, 1975-2007

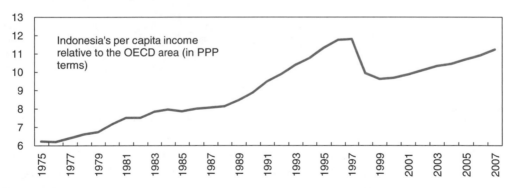

StatLink ▨▧ http://dx.doi.org/10.1787/414540160708

Source: OECD (*MEI database*), World Bank (*World Development Indicators*) and OECD calculations.

grown quite strongly in the post-crisis period.[4] As for the other components of supply, the share of agriculture in GDP is trending down, but it continues to account for the bulk of employment (discussed in Chapter 3).[5] Consistent with a pick-up in private consumption, growth in the services sector has been particularly brisk over the last five years. These trends suggest that the sectors producing non-tradable goods have become increasingly more dynamic relative to those specialising in tradables, including agriculture, forestry and fisheries, mining and manufacturing.

Table 1.1. **Indonesia: Selected macroeconomic indicators, 2001-07**

	2001	2002	2003	2004	2005	2006	2007
Supply and demand							
GDP (in current trillion *rupiah*)	1 684.3	1 897.8	2 045.9	2 273.1	2 785.0	3 339.5	3 957.4
GDP (in current USD billion)	164.1	203.8	238.5	254.3	287.0	364.6	432.8
GDP per capita (in USD PPP)	2 530.9	2 655.5	2 803.9	2 988.0	3 209.5	3 454.4	...
GDP growth rate (real, in per cent)	3.8	4.3	5.0	4.9	5.7	5.5	6.3
GDP growth rate (real, in per capita, in per cent)	2.4	2.9	3.6	3.5	4.3	4.5	5.1
Supply (real growth rate, in per cent)							
Agriculture	4.1	2.7	4.8	2.1	2.2	3.4	3.5
Mining	0.3	0.5	−0.4	−4.9	3.1	1.8	2.0
Manufacturing	3.3	5.9	4.7	6.4	4.6	4.6	4.7
Services[1]	5.0	4.7	6.6	7.2	8.0	7.4	8.9
Demand (real growth rate, in per cent)							
Private consumption	3.5	3.8	3.9	5.0	4.0	3.2	5.0
Public consumption	7.5	13.0	10.1	4.0	6.7	9.7	3.9
Gross fixed investment	6.5	2.2	3.5	14.1	10.9	2.5	9.2
Exports	0.6	−1.0	8.0	11.1	16.4	9.6	8.0
Imports	4.2	−4.0	2.5	25.6	16.7	9.2	8.9
Public finances (central government, in per cent of GDP)							
Revenue	18.3	16.4	17.0	17.8	17.8	19.1	17.9
Expenditure	20.7	17.7	18.7	18.6	18.3	20.1	19.1
Overall balance	−2.5	−1.3	−1.7	−1.0	−0.5	−1.0	−1.2
Gross debt (general government)	75.0	65.8	60.6	56.1	45.5	39.2	35.0
Exchange rate, interest rate and prices							
Exchange rate (*rupiah* per USD, end-period)	10 255	9 318	8 572	8 941	9 713	9 167	9 140
Short-term interest rate (One-month SBI rate, in per cent)	17.6	12.9	8.3	7.4	12.8	9.8	8.0
CPI inflation (in per cent, end-of-period)	12.5	9.9	5.2	6.5	17.1	6.6	6.6
GDP deflator (in per cent)	16.7	8.1	2.7	5.9	15.9	13.6	11.5
Balance of payments (in USD billion)							
Current account balance	6.9	7.8	8.1	1.6	0.3	10.8	10.4
In per cent of GDP	4.2	3.9	3.4	0.6	0.1	2.9	2.4
Trade balance	22.7	23.5	24.6	20.2	17.5	29.7	21.7
Exports	57.4	59.2	64.1	70.8	87.0	103.5	118.0
Imports	34.7	35.7	39.5	50.6	69.5	73.9	85.3
International reserves (gross)	28.0	32.0	36.3	36.3	34.7	42.6	56.9
Outstanding external debt	133.1	131.3	135.4	137.0	130.7	128.7	136.6
In per cent of GDP	80.7	65.7	57.0	53.4	45.3	34.9	31.2

1. Includes electricity, gas, water and construction.
Source: World Bank (*World Development Indicators*), Ministry of Finance, BPS, Bloomberg and OECD calculations.

Indonesia's per capita income gap relative to the OECD average (measured in purchasing power parity terms) has narrowed since the sharp drop induced by the crisis. Rapid growth during 1989-96 led to a swift convergence in relative income levels, a trend that was interrupted by the financial crisis. Indonesia's relative income level nevertheless remains low and has yet to reach the pre-crisis peak of about 12% of the OECD average. This income gap illustrates the scope for catching-up in relative standards of living in the years to come. For example, if the economy grew by 8.5% per year during 2006-30 (about 7.5% in per capita terms), as envisaged in *Visi Indonesia 2030* (Box 1.1), and considering that potential growth in the OECD area is at most 2.5% per year (about 1.7% in per capita terms) on average, Indonesia's income level would rise to about 40% of the OECD average in 2030. This is comparable to the current relative income level of the less affluent OECD member countries, such as Mexico.

> ### Box 1.1. **Visi Indonesia 2030: The main elements**
>
> Visi Indonesia 2030's main objectives are: i) to place Indonesia among the world's five largest economies, with GDP per capita in the neighbourhood of USD 18 000 (for a population of 285 million people), and among the top 30 countries in terms of human development (on the basis of the United Nation's HDI index), and ii) to ensure the inclusion of 30 Indonesian companies among the Fortune 500 Companies. Attainment of these objectives should also be consistent with a sustainable management of the nation's natural resources, especially with regards to the need to secure the supply of food, energy and water. Including Indonesia among the world's top ten tourist destinations is another complementary objective.
>
> The document describes Indonesia's projected growth trajectory in three separate phases: restructuring, with growth initially in the range of 5-7% per year; acceleration, with annual growth at about 9-11% in real terms; and sustainability, with a slowdown in annual growth to about 7-9%. The average real GDP growth rate during 2006-30 would need to be 8.5% per year, for an inflation rate of 3%, which is consistent with that of the country's main trading partners, and population growth at about 1.1% per year. During restructuring, growth would be driven by the acquisition of foreign technology, which would foster growth during the acceleration phase, especially in manufacturing and then in services, so as to achieve a sustainable growth path over the longer term. Growth should be consistent with a reduction in the incidence of poverty to about 4% of the population from nearly 18% in 2006.
>
> This growth pattern would be consistent with a decline in the share of agriculture in GDP and a strengthening of the services sector, with a steady GDP share of manufacturing. The take-off and sustainability of growth would require durable increases in productivity per worker, especially in agriculture and manufacturing. Technological development and innovation are considered to be keys to achieving this goal. The private sector would be the main source of dynamism in the economy.
>
> Productivity-driven growth will depend on improvements in the population's average educational attainment. To this end, both access to, and the quality of, education services will need to improve at all levels of enrolment. Some emphasis will need to be placed on higher education as a vehicle for innovation during the acceleration phase. Also, efforts to enhance the competitiveness of the Indonesian economy would need to focus on improving the investment climate and governance, and to create synergies between the private sector and the government.

Input accumulation versus productivity gains

Input accumulation, rather than productivity enhancement, has been the main driver of growth in Indonesia. On the basis of the estimates reported in Annex 1.A1 using national-accounts data, the accumulation of labour and physical capital accounted for most of the estimated trend GDP growth before the crisis. Gains in total factor productivity (TFP) – the efficiency with which the factors of production are used to produce output – accounted for only about one-quarter of the estimated 6% trend GDP growth rate during 1990-96. The contribution of TFP growth nevertheless appears to be rising: it accounted for about 35-40% of the estimated 4% trend GDP growth during 2000-07. These national-accounts-based calculations are by and large consistent with estimations using sectoral or enterprise-level information. There are large variations in estimates, depending on data sources and methodology used, but recent empirical analysis has emphasised a recovery in TFP growth over the last few years (Box 1.2).

Box 1.2. **Growth accounting in Indonesia: A summary of the literature**

Although methodological differences among the empirical studies lead to a broad range of estimates, there is general agreement that growth has been based predominantly on the accumulation of inputs, in particular physical capital. Sector- and firm-level analysis on the basis of Indonesia's annual Industrial Survey (*Statistik Industri*) yields higher estimates of TFP growth in the pre-crisis period than those obtained from national-accounts data.

Economy-wide evidence

Van der Eng (2007) reports an increase in TFP growth after 2000 to about 2% per year during 2000-06 on the basis of a production function using education-augmented employment and varying labour shares. Prior to 1997, TFP growth was positive but contributed only marginally to output growth. Since 2000, however, TFP growth has risen and accounted for a higher share of output growth.

TFP growth based on economy-wide data tends to be underestimated in Indonesia, because the labour share measured from the national accounts is exceedingly low at 0.2, against an average of 0.6-0.7 in the OECD area. Attempts have been made to re-estimate labour income (*e.g.* Sarel, 1997), suggesting a higher share of about two-third of national income. The estimates reported by Vial (2006) based on firm-level data in manufacturing during 1988-95 point to an elasticity of value added to labour in the neighbourhood of 0.74, which tends to be higher in more labour-intensive sectors. This discrepancy between the estimated and national accounts measures of labour shares suggests that the share of wages in value added is indeed severely underreported.

Sectoral evidence

Timmer (1999) and Aswicahyono and Hill (2002) are among the forerunners to growth accounting using Indonesian manufacturing data. Both studies report an increase in TFP growth after economic liberalisation in the mid-1980s relative to the 1970s. Timmer (1999) estimates that TFP gains accounted for about one-fifth of growth in manufacturing value added during 1975-95. The contribution of inter-sectoral input reallocation is estimated to have been low over the period. Aswicahyono and Hill (2002) find that TFP accounted for about one-third of industrial growth during 1984-93, essentially due to within-sector productivity gains. TFP levels across sectors also converged more rapidly over the period.

Warr (2006) decomposes growth between factor accumulation and improvements in TFP and the latter between the weighted average of sectoral productivity levels and the efficiency effect of factor movements among sectors with varying levels of productivity. The decomposition exercise is carried out for the period 1980-2002. The results show that 93% of growth in the pre-crisis period (1980-96) was attributable to factor accumulation alone. TFP growth turned negative in the immediate post-crisis period. Contrary to previous findings, however, the reallocation effect is particularly strong in explaining TFP growth in both pre- and post-crisis periods.

Estimates of TFP growth in agriculture also suggest that most of the increase in output stems from input accumulation (Fuglie, 2004). Most of the growth in TFP appears to have taken place during 1968-92; therefore, the lack of productivity growth thereafter cannot be explained entirely by the financial crisis.

Of course, TFP estimates are sensitive to modelling assumptions, data quality (especially with regards to the computation of the physical capital stock), the choice of sectoral aggregation techniques, and the selection of deflators, among other issues. The fact that the industrial survey, on which most current estimates are based, does not report capital stock, and that the investment series are considered to suffer from considerable underreporting (Timmer, 1999) are important sources of concern regarding the reliability of existing estimates.

TFP growth is estimated to have been affected positively by structural reform, especially those changes that have enhanced trade openness. Indonesia went through a period of economic liberalisation in the mid-1980s, including a gradual reduction in trade protection (Figure 1.3 and Box 1.3). These reforms have contributed to raising productivity in non-oil manufacturing relative to the 1970s, when policies were more interventionist, and the country's trade and investment regimes were more restrictive (Aswicahyono and Hill, 2002). In general, increasing trade openness is expected to boost TFP growth not only through heightened competition with imported goods, but also as a result of knowledge spillovers and technological progress embodied in imported capital goods and intermediate inputs. This potential stimulus to the diffusion of technological progress is particularly important in Indonesia, given the low level of R&D carried out by the private sector (discussed below). Increased trade openness was also accompanied by a gradual decline in export concentration for both markets and goods, including for non-oil products (Figure 1.4). But the trend in export concentration appears to have levelled off since the financial crisis.

The effect of trade liberalisation on productivity appears to have been strongest as a result of lower tariff protection for goods used as industrial inputs, rather than final goods. This is confirmed by empirical evidence for the manufacturing sector (Amiti and Konings, 2005). It can be argued that lower tariffs on imported inputs are productivity-enhancing because of product variety and quality effects. But the comparatively weaker effect of trade liberalisation on productivity due to lower tariffs on final goods might suggest the presence of barriers to competition. This is because, for a more liberal trade regime to contribute to efficiency gains, it needs to foster competition in domestic markets.[6] Based on this empirical finding, it can be argued that product-market regulations may have failed to ensure competition between domestic and foreign producers as the country's trade regime was liberalised.

Figure 1.3. **Trade protection, 1989-2006**
MFN tariffs (unweighted averages)

A. By type

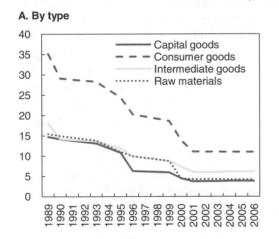

B. By sector

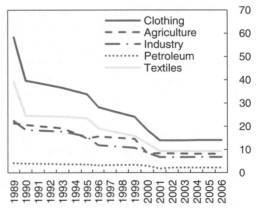

StatLink ⬛⬛⬛ http://dx.doi.org/10.1787/414586677443

Source: UNCTAD-TRAINS and OECD calculations.

Box 1.3. **Indonesia's trade regime and performance: An overview**

Trade regime

Indonesia is a fairly open economy. Import tariffs have been declining steadily since the 1980s. The average unweighted MFN tariff was 7% in 2006 (6.1% if trade-weighted). The authorities are committed to reducing average tariffs further by 2010. By then, 87% of tariff lines will be either 5% or 10%. There is, however, an exemption list of products subject to import duties of 35% or more, which accounts for about 6% of all tariff lines. These products will not be subject to lower rates until 2020.

At about 3-4%, Indonesia's effective import tariff, defined as the ratio of revenue from customs duties to imports, is much lower than the average MFN tariff rate. This is essentially because of Indonesia's commitments to the ASEAN Free Trade Agreement (AFTA); accordingly, the most common effective preferential tariff lines have rates ranging between 0 and 5%. At the same time, a substantial proportion of imported intermediate goods enter duty-free under Indonesia's various export facilitation programmes.

Despite comparatively low tariffs, Indonesia's trade regime also includes a number of non-tariff barriers. They are related predominantly to a range of agricultural products, including rice, sugar, wheat flour, shrimps and cloves, as well as motor vehicles, electronic components and textiles, among other items. Non-tariff protection has increased since 2001, and anti-dumping measures are alleged to have been used as a protectionist instrument.

The liberalisation of Indonesia's trade regime over the years is unlikely to be reversed. But protectionist pressures sometimes emerge, reflecting to a certain extent different policy priorities among the government agencies and ministries in charge of setting tariff and non-tariff instruments. Import tariffs are under the purview of the Ministry of Finance, which is a proponent of trade openness, while non-tariff barriers are often set by line ministries, such as Agriculture and Industry, which tend to be more protectionist (Basri and Soesastro, 2005).

Trade performance

Despite a relatively open trade regime, Indonesia' actual openness, measured as the ratio of imports and exports to GDP, is much lower than in regional comparator countries. At about 51% of GDP, Indonesia's trade ratio compares unfavourably with the average of 130% of GDP for the ASEAN countries during 2000-07, although Indonesia is much larger than those other countries. In addition, Indonesia's market share has stagnated at nearly 1% of world trade, while those of other Asian countries have risen since the 1997-98 financial crisis. This export stagnation is especially disturbing in the case of labour-intensive goods and natural resources, in which Indonesia has a comparative advantage.

There is potential for raising Indonesia's trade. Controlling for size, economic development and location, the empirical evidence reported by Jain-Chandra (2007) shows that actual import and export flows are significantly below the levels implied by standard gravity models. This gap suggests that there is considerable latent demand for Indonesian exports and scope for raising imports. Supply constraints, discussed elsewhere in this *Economic Assessment*, may create obstacles for higher trade. But comparative advantages and specialisation patterns also matter.

Figure 1.4. **Export concentration, 1979-2005**[1]

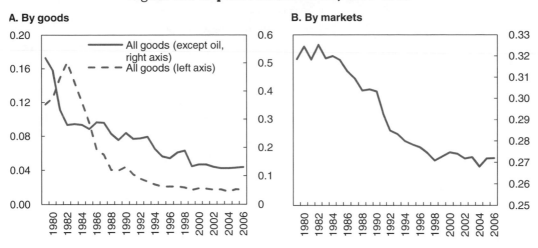

1. Export concentration is defined as $C = \sum_i \left(\dfrac{X_i}{X} \right)^2$, where X denotes total exports and i denotes export markets or goods.

StatLink http://dx.doi.org/10.1787/414620775105

Source: COMTRADE and OECD calculations.

Efficiency gains can also arise from competition in foreign markets. Exporting firms tend to be more efficient than domestic firms, because they compete abroad. This is confirmed by empirical evidence for Indonesia: analysis based on enterprise-level data shows that exporting firms tend to be more productive and to grow faster than non-exporting firms (Sjöholm, 1999a and 1999b). Cross-country experience also suggests that exporting firms tend to be more innovative than their counterparts that do not export. This association between innovation, productivity and export orientation is important, because it underscores the logic of integrating – and maximising synergies – among policies in the areas of innovation and trade competitiveness.

FDI also contributes to productivity growth. Foreign-owned or controlled enterprises tend to be more efficient than their locally-owned counterparts. This is because they have superior firm-specific assets arising from the use of more modern technologies, best management practices and know-how, and easier access to global distribution, marketing and production networks. This hypothesis is borne out by Indonesian data. Evidence at the enterprise level for the manufacturing sector suggests that value added per employee is indeed higher in foreign-owned or controlled firms, taking account of scale effects in production (Takii and Ramstetter, 2005). The share of foreign-owned enterprises in value added has risen steadily over time, including in the aftermath of the 1997-98 crisis, to reach about 36% on average in 2000-05 (with 22% of employment).[7] The sectors with the largest presence of foreign-owned or controlled firms are electric, electronic and precision machinery.

Labour productivity has risen at a relatively modest pace in manufacturing since 1997-98. Industrial-survey data for manufacturing enterprises with at least 20 employees show that labour productivity grew on average by about 1.3% per year during 1999-2005 (Figure 1.5). Productivity gains have been particularly high in sectors such as machinery and equipment, and productivity gaps between enterprises of different sizes appear to have persisted over time. It should be recognised, however, that these trends may overestimate productivity growth to the extent that smaller enterprises, which account for

Figure 1.5. **Labour productivity in manufacturing, 1999-2005**[1]

1999 = 100

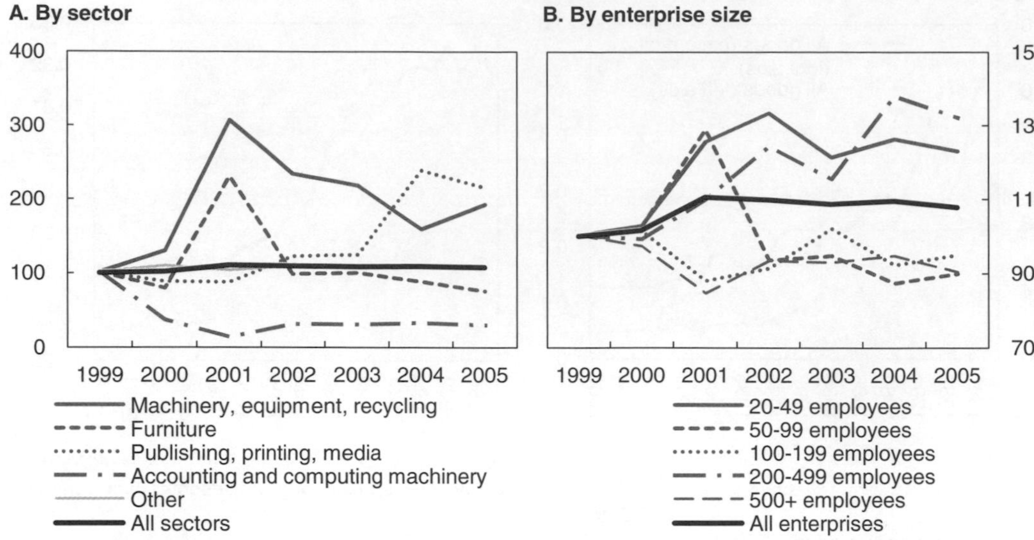
A. By sector
400
300
200
100
0
1999 2000 2001 2002 2003 2004 2005
Machinery, equipment, recycling
Furniture
Publishing, printing, media
Accounting and computing machinery
Other
All sectors
B. By enterprise size
150
130
110
90
70
1999 2000 2001 2002 2003 2004 2005
20-49 employees
50-99 employees
100-199 employees
200-499 employees
500+ employees
All enterprises

StatLink http://dx.doi.org/10.1787/414652628151

1. Deflated by the GDP deflator.

Source: BPS (*Statistik Industri*) and OECD calculations.

the bulk of employment in Indonesia, including unregistered businesses, are excluded. Labour productivity is likely to have risen at an even slower pace in those enterprises.

The bulk of labour productivity growth can be attributed to firm dynamics. This is the case when entry of more productive firms displaces their less productive counterparts, and resources (labour and capital) can be reallocated to more productive uses. Empirical evidence using enterprise-level data shows that the effect of entry and exit on productivity was particularly strong for smaller enterprises over the period 1994-2000 (ter Wengel and Rodriguez, 2006). However, firm dynamics appear to have changed over time. Entry rates do not seem to have recovered after the crisis (Narjoko, 2006). Smaller firms are growing more slowly, and most output growth is now coming from existing firms, rather than from new entrants. Sector-level data shows that net entry has been negative in selected sectors, including textiles, clothing and footwear, wood products and non-metallic minerals, in which Indonesia has a comparative advantage, but positive in basic metals and electronics. Conversely, patterns in plant expansions and contractions do not seem to have changed after the crisis, although there are variations across sectors. These findings underscore the scope for productivity enhancement through regulatory reform aimed at lowering entry costs, such as pro-business registration and licensing procedures, and facilitating exit, through effective bankruptcy legislation and well functioning legal and court systems (discussed in Chapter 2).

The macroeconomic policy setting

There is broad agreement that a stable macroeconomy is an essential framework condition for sustained growth. Indonesia's policy framework has evolved considerably over the years, and the country's macroeconomic performance has improved.

 OECD ECONOMIC SURVEYS: INDONESIA: ECONOMIC ASSESMENT – ISBN 978-92-64-04805-8 – © OECD 2008

Fiscal policy

Fiscal policy has been conducted in an increasingly decentralised manner. The process of decentralisation that was launched in 2001 put the local governments at the helm of service delivery (Box 1.4). Resolute central government control over sub-national finances, especially in the areas of budget making, financial management and investment, has prevented financial imbalances from emerging and endangering overall macroeconomic stability. This is particularly remarkable in a country with sizeable vertical imbalances in intergovernmental fiscal relations, which are financed predominantly through block transfers from the centre. In such an environment, international experience suggests that decentralisation often results in fiscal disarray, especially in countries with comparatively weak fiscal institutions (de Mello, 2000). Another achievement on which Indonesia should be commended is the actual implementation of decentralisation in 2001, a complex process that required considerable coordination efforts to prevent disruptions in service delivery.

Fiscal performance has improved over the years. Tax revenue has risen steadily, especially from the income tax and, to a lesser extent, the value-added tax (VAT) (Table 1.2). Revenue from taxes on international trade is coming down in relation to GDP, reflecting essentially a gradual reduction in import tariffs (discussed above). Efforts are under way to strengthen tax administration, especially with respect to the protection of taxpayers' rights[8] and the administration of VAT refunds; to alleviate the income tax burden on businesses by reducing marginal tax rates; and to broaden the VAT base. Decisive action has been taken to stamp out corruption in customs and tax administration, including by the dismissal of senior government officials and a significant increase in compensation for civil servants working in those agencies.

At the same time, there have been important changes in the composition of expenditure. A reduction in interest payments since the financial crisis has created room in the central government budget for hiking capital spending. Also, transfers to the provinces and local governments have increased since 2001 in tandem with decentralisation, which has also led to a gradual decrease in central government spending on payroll, because of the devolution of formerly deconcentrated personnel to sub-national jurisdictions.

Despite successive reductions, especially in 2001-02 and 2005, price subsidies for fuel and electricity continue to weigh heavily on the budget. Despite an increase in domestic prices by nearly 30% in May, fuel subsidies are projected to account for almost 20% of spending in 2008, up from about 13% in 2007, owing to high international oil prices. Fuel subsidies correspond to the transfers from the central government to the State-owned oil company (*Pertamina*) to cover the losses the company incurs when the domestic price of fuel is kept below international prices. Electricity subsidies, which also arise from maintenance of domestic prices below their market-clearing level, are also costly to the budget.[9] The authorities have reiterated on several occasions their intention to eliminate these subsidies, but no date has yet been set. Efforts to introduce explicit mechanisms for adjusting domestic fuel prices, such as in 2001-02, have faced political opposition, especially in periods of rising international oil prices.

Fuel price subsidies are undesirable for a number of reasons. *First*, they benefit the well-off more than vulnerable individuals. Official estimates show that nearly two-thirds of subsidies on fuels accrue to the richest 40% of the population. The electricity subsidies that

Box 1.4. **Fiscal decentralisation in Indonesia: Achievements and challenges**

Following the demise of the Suharto regime in 1998, Indonesia launched an ambitious fiscal decentralisation programme in 2001. Decentralisation allowed for increasing demands for policymaking autonomy at the sub-national level to be met in a country that is characterised by considerable economic, geographic, religious and ethnic diversity. Indonesia is the world's largest archipelago State and one of the most spatially diverse nations in its resource endowments, population settlements, location of economic activity, ecology and ethnicity. There are in total 350 identified ethnic groups. In the early 2000s, per capita regional product in the richest province, East Kalimantan, was around 16 times that of the poorest, Maluku (Annex 1.A2).

The institutional framework for decentralisation was consolidated in Laws No. 22 (on regional governance) and No. 25 (on intergovernmental fiscal relations) of 1999. Complementary legislation was issued in 2004 (Law No. 32 of 2004) to strengthen central government control over local government finances and to clarify expenditure assignments between the provinces and the local governments. The main features of Indonesian decentralisation are as follows:

● **A focus on local, rather than middle-tier, governments in service delivery.** Several expenditure assignments, especially in the social area, were decentralised to the local governments (*kabupaten/kota*). Local governments were also granted political autonomy, and efforts have been made to boost accountability of locally elected leaders and legislatures. Local governments now account for almost two-thirds of consolidated government spending, nearly double the pre-decentralisation share.

● **Significant vertical and horizontal imbalances in intergovernmental fiscal relations.** Local governments have limited taxing autonomy: income and property tax revenue is collected by the centre and transferred to the local governments on a derivation basis. The bulk of local government revenue comes from a general allocation grant (DAU, *dana alokasi umum*),[1] followed by the sharing of oil and gas revenue (SDA) and earmarked or conditional transfers (DAK, *dana alokasi khusus*), which are used to finance predominantly capital outlays. Own revenue accounts for less than 10% of local government revenue. Decentralisation exacerbated horizontal inequality among the local governments, because the sharing of revenue from the exploitation of natural resources is limited to the oil- and gas-rich provinces, and the scope for equalisation through the general allocation grant on the basis of estimated fiscal capacity and expenditure needs is limited.

● **Central government financial control.** The central government retains control over the regional governments (provinces and local governments) in areas related to tax policy (by setting tax bases and ranges for rates), budget making (local budgets need to be submitted to and approved by the central government), financial management (there are constraints on local government borrowing and debt management) and investment programmes, including in devolved sectors, such as education, health care and infrastructure development.

The main achievements of "big-bang" decentralisation in 2001 are as follows:

● **Smooth implementation.** Legal uncertainty and the need to decentralise a large number of personnel and assets to the provinces and local governments posed considerable risk of disruption in service delivery in the wake of decentralisation. Nevertheless, disruption was minimal, despite serious administrative and capacity constraints at the local level.

Box 1.4. **Fiscal decentralisation in Indonesia: Achievements and challenges**
(cont.)

- **Preservation of macroeconomic stability.** The decentralisation of expenditure mandates and the design of revenue sharing and transfer systems posed risks for macroeconomic financial management. Nevertheless, revenue sharing was guided by a "revenue-follows-expenditure" principle, which prevented the creation of unfunded mandates, although expenditure needs were not carefully assessed at the time of decentralisation. Legal constraints imposed on sub-national financial operations, including on borrowing, also minimised financial risks. Since 2004, there has been greater control by the centre on regional government budget making and personnel management.

Despite these achievements, there are important challenges to be addressed.

- **Capacity constraints.** The demands imposed by decentralisation have put considerable strain on the central government, particularly in the areas of budget making and more recently personnel management. Delays in the approval of local government budgets are not infrequent, which disrupts the implementation of local infrastructure projects, for example, as discussed in Chapter 2. At the local government level, capacity constraints are concentrated in service delivery. It is estimated that regions have been building up savings over the recent past that amounted to some 70 trillion *rupiah* (2% of GDP) at the beginning of 2006 (World Bank, 2006).

- **Creation of local taxes and levies.**[2] Such levies are often created in an extra-legal manner (*i.e.* without the review and approval by the central government, as required by law), despite the issuance of Law No. 34 of 2006, which sets out a "positive list" of allowable taxes, together with prescribed rate ranges. This proliferation of local levies has resulted in institutional uncertainties that have affected the business climate adversely, as discussed in Chapter 2. The proliferation of such levies has also created a fertile ground for corruption.

- **Scope for horizontal equalisation in the grant system.** There is a trade-off between increased emphasis on the financing of local government wage costs on the basis of general allocation transfers (DAU) after 2004 and the scope for equalisation through grant arrangements. In addition, for the equalisation component of the grant system to be effective, information is needed on local government fiscal capacity and expenditure needs to be reliable and timely, instead of the proxies currently used.

- **Proliferation of local jurisdictions.** The number of local governments rose from 314 in 1998 to 440 at end-2005. Also, five provinces were created, raising their number to 33. Legal constraints on the creation of new jurisdictions are lax and incentives are strong, given the reliance of local governments on financing from the centre, as well as bureaucratic and political rent seeking in some cases.[3]

1. DAU is financed through a fixed share of central government net revenue (currently 26%), of which 90% is allocated to the local governments on derivation and, to a much lesser extent, equalisation bases, and the remainder is allocated to the provinces. Although DAU allocations are intended to be formula-based, they are still guided in part by historical budgeting on the basis of pre-decentralisation appropriations for the formerly deconcentrated personnel and assets that have subsequently been decentralised to the regional governments. There has been less emphasis on equalisation and more on financing local government wage bill since 2004. See Hofman *et al.* (2006) for more information.
2. See Lewis (2006) for more information.
3. See Fitrani *et al.* (2005) for more information.

Table 1.2. **Budget operations: Central government, 1990-2007**

In per cent of GDP

	1990	1995	2000	2005	2006	2007
Revenue and grants	18.1	14.2	14.8	17.8	19.1	17.9
Tax	9.4	9.7	8.3	12.5	12.2	12.4
Income tax	3.5	4.2	4.1	6.3	6.3	6.0
Value-added tax (VAT)	3.5	4.2	2.8	5.0	5.0	4.9
International trade	...	...	1.3	1.3	1.3	1.1
Other	3.5	3.7	2.5	3.6	3.7	3.9
Non-tax	1.2	0.6	0.5	0.5	0.4	0.5
Grants	1.2	1.2	1.2	2.0	1.9	1.9
Expenditure	17.1	13.0	15.9	18.3	20.1	19.1
Current	7.7	5.7	11.7	10.7	10.2	11.1
Personnel	3.0	2.6	2.1	2.0	2.2	2.3
Goods and services	0.8	1.0	0.7	1.2	1.4	1.4
Interest payments	2.1	1.3	3.6	2.1	2.4	2.0
Subsidies	1.5	0.0	4.5	4.3	3.2	3.8
of which: fuel	1.5	0.0	3.9	3.4	1.9	2.1
Other	0.2	0.7	0.8	1.1	1.1	1.6
Development outlays[1]	6.4	4.3	1.9	2.2	3.1	1.6
Intergovernmental transfers	3.0	3.1	2.4	5.4	6.8	6.4
Overall balance	1.0	1.2	−1.2	−0.5	−1.0	−1.2
Memorandum items:						
Financing						
Domestic sources	−1.4	−0.2	0.4	0.8	1.7	1.8
Bank	−1.4	−0.6	−0.9	−0.1	0.6	0.4
Non-bank	0.0	0.3	1.4	0.9	1.1	1.5
Privatisation	0.0	0.0	0.0	0.0	0.0	0.0
Recovery of bank assets	0.0	0.0	1.4	0.2	0.1	0.1
Bond assurances	0.0	0.3	0.0	0.8	1.1	1.4
Foreign sources	0.3	−1.0	0.7	−0.4	−0.8	−0.6
Gross debt	42.4	30.8	83.8	45.5	39.2	35.0

1. Comprises outlays on capital and social assistance from 2005.
Source: Ministry of Finance, World Bank (*World Development Indicators*) and OECD calculations.

are not capped at low consumption capacity have also been shown to be rather regressive (World Bank, 2007). *Second*, they pose an undue financial burden on the State-owned utility companies, which are prevented from pursuing their commercial objectives independently of the government's social policies. *Third*, they have an adverse impact on the environment by keeping the price of fossil fuels artificially low, thereby discouraging conservation and a search for alternative sources of energy. *Finally*, by putting pressure on the budget, these subsidies run counter to ongoing efforts to allocate a rising share of budgetary resources to infrastructure investment, human capital accumulation and social protection programmes.

Consistent with improving fiscal performance and growth, public indebtedness has come down from about 84% of GDP in 2000 to 35% in 2007. The public debt ratio rose alarmingly in the immediate aftermath of the 1997-98 crisis, owing principally to the costs accruing to the budget from the government's blanket deposit guarantee scheme and the issuance of recapitalisation bonds to rescue the failing banking and corporate sectors, totalling about 740 trillion *rupiah* in 1998-99 (about one-half of GDP in 1999). However, owing to fiscal restraint, public debt has fallen quickly as a proportion of GDP since 2001.[10]

A Fiscal Law (Law No. 17) was introduced in 2003, capping budget deficits at 2% of GDP and the public debt at 60% of GDP.

There is fairly widespread agreement that, with favourable public debt dynamics, Indonesia is likely to enjoy a comfortable fiscal position over the longer term. A further gradual reduction in public indebtedness is expected to continue to alleviate the financial burden of debt service. At the same time, efforts to cut back price subsidies would create further room in the budget to reallocate appropriations in favour of more meritorious, growth-enhancing programmes. These trends are welcome, because a strengthening of social protection, especially through targeted income transfers to vulnerable households (discussed in Chapter 3), as well as rising demand for social services, including education and health care (see below), will probably account for a growing share of the budget.

Monetary policy

Monetary policy has been conducted within a fully-fledged inflation-targeting regime since July 2005, when monetary targeting was formally abandoned (Box 1.5). Annual inflation targets had been announced since 2000, and legislation was issued in 1999 (and revised in 2004) granting Bank Indonesia independence. It is therefore too soon to ascertain the extent to which the change in the policy regime has affected macroeconomic outcomes in a discernible manner. Credibility was enhanced by Bank Indonesia's resolute response to an upsurge in inflation in 2005-06, when it pre-emptively raised the policy interest rate to tackle the second-round effect of the adjustment in fuel prices from feeding through to headline inflation (Figure 1.6). The inflation outlook nevertheless began to deteriorate towards end-2007 owing to rising food and unsubsidised fuel prices, and worsening inflation expectations. The policy interest rate was raised by 50-basis points in total in May and June 2008 to 8.5% following a 25-basis-point cut in December 2007. A further tightening is expected in the course of the year in response to the sharp increase in domestic fuel prices in mid-May. Decisive action in this area is essential for anchoring inflation expectations over the coming months and continuing to build credibility in the policy regime.

Inflation is currently higher in Indonesia than in the country's main trading partners. At nearly 14%, Indonesia's average consumer-price inflation during 1995-2007 is well above the 2% average of its trading partners. Inflation is also more volatile in Indonesia: the coefficient of variation of inflation during 1995-2007 is about 1.1, against nearly 0.4 for the average of the country's main trading partners. The most important consideration in this area is that a persistent inflation differential is detrimental to the competitiveness of Indonesian exports if the nominal exchange rate fails to adjust. The government has signalled its commitment to inflation convergence by setting gradually decreasing the inflation targets for 2008-10, from 4-6% in 2008 to 3-5% in the medium term.

A floating exchange-rate regime is serving Indonesia well. It has allowed the central bank greater flexibility to conduct monetary policy. Exchange-rate flexibility also has the advantage of allowing adverse external shocks to be absorbed at a lower output loss than in the case of managed or fixed regimes. The central bank has intervened periodically in the foreign-exchange market, especially in periods when the exchange rate has appreciated and concern has emerged about export competitiveness. Until recently, a declining interest-rate differential with respect to global markets had put some downward pressure on the *rupiah*.

Box 1.5. **Inflation targeting in Indonesia**

Bank Indonesia has set and announced explicit inflation targets as its ultimate monetary policy objectives since 2000, following the enactment of the central bank law in 1999.* The law was subsequently amended in 2004, and the inflation target was set by the government in coordination with the central bank at 5-7% in 2005, 4.5-6.5% in 2006 and 4-7% in 2007. These targets were revised upwards in March 2006 to 7-9% in 2006 and to 5-7% in 2007 and set at 4-6% in 2008.

Both the definition of the price index used for targeting inflation and the level of inflation to be targeted have changed over the years. BI announced its first annual target for CPI inflation at the beginning of 2000 for the period 2000-01 excluding administered prices. The target was set for full CPI inflation in 2002. The central bank nevertheless emphasized core inflation, which excluded administered and volatile food prices, when formulating monetary policy. In addition to setting the annual targets, the central bank also announced in 2002 its commitment to bring CPI inflation down to a 6-7% range within five years as a medium-term inflation objective. This long-term target was adjusted upwards in 2006 to the 7-9% range in response to the fuel-price hike, but was subsequently lowered to 5-7% from 2007.

As in other inflation-targeting emerging-market economies, the announcement of targets for inflation coexisted with monetary targeting during an initial transition phase. BI used base money as its operational target until July 2005, but the instability of money demand and the difficulty of pursuing two separate targets led the central bank to focus solely on the pursuit of its inflation target.

The policy interest rate is the BI Rate, the rate of return on the one-month Bank Indonesia Certificate (SBI). Several facilities are in place for short-term lending and liquidity withdrawal. In addition, to ensure stability in the money-market rate, BI has provided a standing facility (corridor) within an 800 basis-point band (300 basis points above the BI Rate and 500 basis points below it). This band was narrowed in early 2008 to 600 basis points (300 basis points above and below the BI Rate).

* See Sarwono (2008) for more information.

A high share of food and administered prices in the consumption-price index (CPI) poses a challenge for the monetary authorities. To a certain extent, this is true for emerging markets in general, which tend to have a higher weight of such items in the CPI than more mature economies. To deal with this problem, BI and the government set up an Inflation Control Taskforce in 2004, whose members are from various line ministries, to propose the inflation target to be set annually, to evaluate the sources of inflationary pressures and their impact on the achievement of the inflation target, to recommend policy options for achieving the inflation target, and to disseminate information on the inflation target and the policy efforts to achieve it.

The banking sector is sound, having recovered in earnest from the financial crisis of 1997-98. Capital-assets and liquid reserves-assets ratios have improved over the years, and the prevalence of non-performing loans has been reduced (Table 1.3). Banking regulations have been tightened since the financial crisis, including through more stringent requirements for loan classification, provisioning, related-party lending, capital adequacy and exchange-rate risk. The blanket deposit guarantee that was put in place at the time of the crisis has now been replaced by more effective financial safety nets, which

Figure 1.6. **Inflation, monetary policy and exchange rates, 2000-08**
In per cent, unless otherwise indicated

A. Inflation and targets

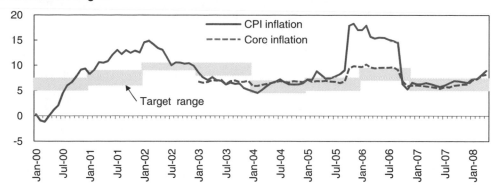

B. Inflation and monetary policy

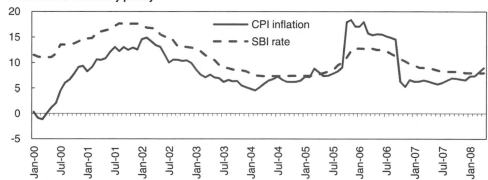

C. Exchange rates

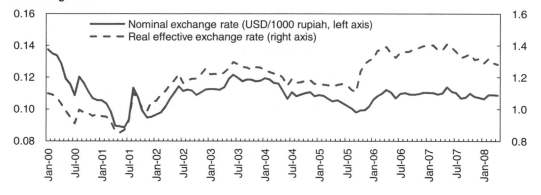

StatLink ⬛⬛ http://dx.doi.org/10.1787/414731445773

Source: Bank Indonesia and OECD calculations.

include lender-of-last-resort operations for systemically important institutions and short-term liquidity facilities for banks, as well as a limited deposit-insurance scheme. Bank Indonesia's supervisory capabilities have also been strengthened. Moreover, there has been considerable consolidation in the banking sector in recent years, a phenomenon that is not yet expected to thwart competitive pressures in the industry. Nevertheless, as discussed in Chapter 2, the non-bank segment remains small, and the banking sector is dominated by State-owned institutions.

Table 1.3. **Indonesia: Selected financial and monetary indicators, 2001-07**

	2001	2002	2003	2004	2005	2006	2007
Financial indicators							
Ratio of bank capital to assets (in per cent)	5.2	8.8	9.6	10.8	10.2	10.7	11.1
Ratio of bank liquid reserves to bank assets	11.1	11.1	12.0	14.1	15.5	15.9	..
Ratio of non-performing loans to gross loans (in per cent)	31.9	24.0	19.4	14.2	14.8	13.1	13.5
Monetary aggregates							
Liquid liabilities (M3, in per cent of GDP)	50.9	48.2	47.0	44.9	43.1	43.1	..
Money and quasi-money (M2, in per cent of GDP)	48.2	47.1	45.3	43.1	40.1	38.6	..
Money and quasi-money (annual, in per cent)	11.9	4.8	7.9	8.9	16.4	14.9	..

Source: World Bank (*World Development Indicators*).

Policy challenges for enhancing growth performance

Boosting human capital accumulation and innovation

Background

Low human capital is an important impediment to productivity enhancement. It constrains technological progress, including both the creation and diffusion of new technologies, and the development of skills-intensive industries. Indonesia's basic indicators of educational attainment have improved but remain sub-par in comparison with OECD countries and regional peers (Table 1.4). Progress in this area, which should not be underestimated, owes much to an ambitious programme that was put in place in the 1970s to build schools and to ensure access to schooling by the population, especially school-age children residing in remote areas. Consistent with these efforts, the increase in educational attainment across age cohorts has been remarkable (Figure 1.7). The share of population with at least lower-secondary education is more than three times as high among younger individuals (25-34 years of age) as for their older counterparts (aged 55-64 years). Notwithstanding this achievement, the performance of Indonesian students on the basis of standardised tests, such as the OECD's Programme for International Student Assessment (PISA), is clearly inferior to that of regional peers and the OECD area.

To a certain extent, Indonesia's low educational attainment and poor performance appear to be associated with a lack of investment in education. Total spending financed from public sources is low in relation to national income, despite some improvement over the years, even with respect to regional comparator countries (Figure 1.8). As an initial step towards remedying this situation, the authorities amended the Constitution in 2002 to introduce a floor for government spending on education at 20% of total expenditure. Budgetary appropriations are therefore expected to rise over time, because current spending remains well below the mandated level.

Consistent with relatively low educational attainment, the human capital embodied in the labour force is also low. Enterprise-level data available from the industrial survey for 1997, the latest year for which comprehensive information is available on the composition of employment in the industrial sector by educational attainment, shows that only about 4% of employees had completed at least higher education, against about 40% for those who have completed upper-secondary education. This is not surprising, given the country's comparatively low tertiary-education attainment rate, which did not vary much across age cohorts.

Table 1.4. **Education and health indicators: Cross-country comparisons, 1990, 2000 and 2005**

	Indonesia			Southeast Asia	OECD
	1990	2000	2005		
Education					
Net enrolment rates (%)					
Primary education	96.6[1]	93.9	95.5	93.2	96.0
Secondary education	39.1[1]	48.6	58.3	68.3	92.3
Tertiary education (gross)	9.2[1]	14.4[2]	17.1	20.4	69.5
Persistence to grade 5, total (% of cohort)	83.6[1]	95.3	89.5[3]	..	..
Repetition rate, primary (% of total enrollment)	9.7[1]	6.2[2]	4.6	1.5	..
Literacy rate (% of population aged 15 and above)	83.6[1]	95.3	89.5[3]	..	..
Males	81.5	..	90.4[3]	90.8	99.1
Females	75.3	..	86.8[3]	86.8	98.9
Health					
Births attended by skilled health staff (% of total)	31.7[1]	64.2[2]	71.5[3]	86.9	..
Pregnant women receiving prenatal care (%)	76.2[1]	..	..	88.6	0.0
Immunisation rates (per cent of children ages 12-23 months)					
DPT	60.0	75.0	70.0	83.7	95.4
Measles	58.0	72.0	72.0	83.4	92.5
Malnutrition prevalence, weight for age (% of children under 5)	..	24.6	..	15.0	..
Incidence of tuberculosis (per 100 000 people)	342.8	269.7	239.2	136.5	16.0
Mortality rate, under age of 5 (per 1 000)	91.0	48.0	36.0	32.7	5.7

1. Refers to 1991.
2. Refers to 2001.
3. Refers to 2004.
Source: World Bank (*World Development Indicators*).

Low human capital also affects a country's potential for innovation, an area where Indonesia fares rather poorly in comparison with OECD countries and regional peers. Input indicators, such as R&D intensity, spending on information and communication technologies, and the share of researchers in the labour force, show that innovation intensity is low (Figure 1.9). To a large extent, R&D activity is affected by the structure of the economy, and spending tends to be comparatively low in natural resource-dependent economies. This is the case even in the OECD area. Moreover, the composition of R&D activity is heavily tilted towards government financing in Indonesia, which accounts for about 80% of the 0.5% of GDP spent on R&D in 2007. As a result, the bulk of scientists and researchers work in public universities and research institutions, rather than in the business sector. This is important, because reliance on public funding is in sharp contrast with the OECD area, where about two-thirds of R&D spending is financed by private sources. Innovation is also affected by low tertiary-educational attainment, which constrains the supply of scientists and skilled labour needed for the development of skills-intensive industries.

As a result of limited innovation activity, it is not surprising that innovation performance, as far as gauged by the number of triadic patents (*i.e.* registered in the European Union, Japan and the United States) and scientific publications held by residents, is also rather unsatisfactory. Indonesia also compares unfavourably with respect to its neighbours in terms of the technological content of its exports. It is important to recognise

Figure 1.7. **Educational attainment and performance: Cross-country comparisons, 2006**

A. Lower-secondary educational attainment by cohort[1]

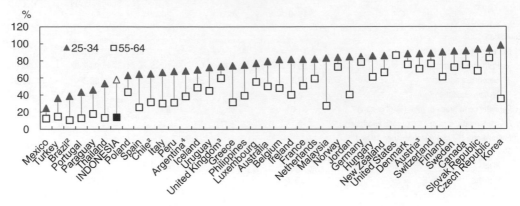

B. PISA score

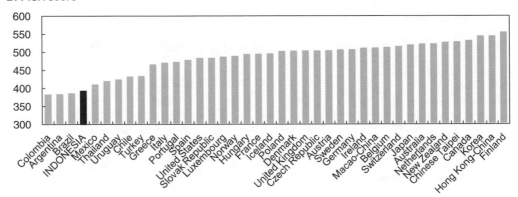

C. Tertiary educational attainment by cohort

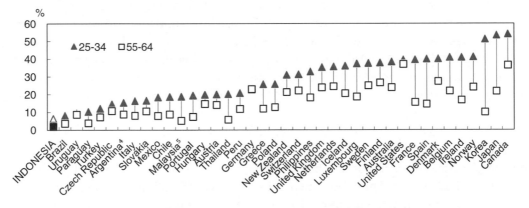

StatLink ᴹˢᴾ http://dx.doi.org/10.1787/414755423170

1. Excludes ISCED 3C short programmes.
2. The year of reference is 2004.
3. Includes some ISCED 3C short programmes.
4. Refers to urban areas.
5. Post-secondary non-tertiary education is included in tertiary education.

Source: OECD (*Education at a Glance*) and UNESCO/UIS WEI.

Figure 1.8. **Expenditure on education: Cross-country comparisons, 2006**

A. Pre-tertiary

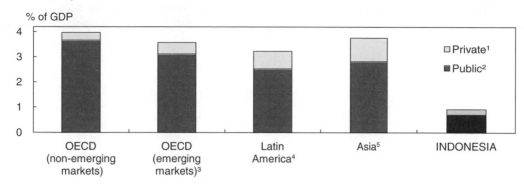

B. Tertiary

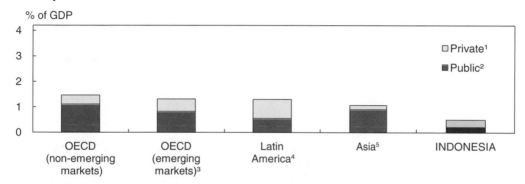

C. Annual expenditure on educational institutions per student relative to GDP per capita

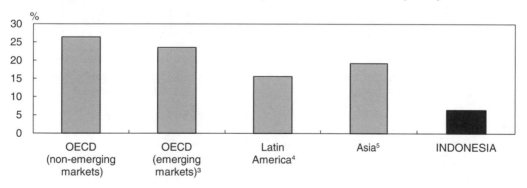

StatLink ⟿ http://dx.doi.org/10.1787/414764330307

1. Net of public subsidies for educational institutions.
2. Includes public subsidies to households attributable to educational institutions and direct expenditure by educational institutions financed from international sources.
3. Includes Czech Republic, Hungary, Korea, Mexico, Slovak Republic and Turkey.
4. Includes Argentina, Brazil (only public spending), Chile, Paraguay, Peru and Uruguay.
5. Includes India, Malaysia, Philippines and Thailand.
Source: OECD (Education at a Glance).

that patents and publications are imperfect output indicators, given that successful innovation outcomes may also result in copyright and other licensing arrangements. But, all in all, on the basis of these conventional metrics, there appears to be plenty of room for improvement as a means of raising productivity in Indonesia through increases in innovation intensity.

Figure 1.9. **Innovation indicators: Cross-country comparisons**

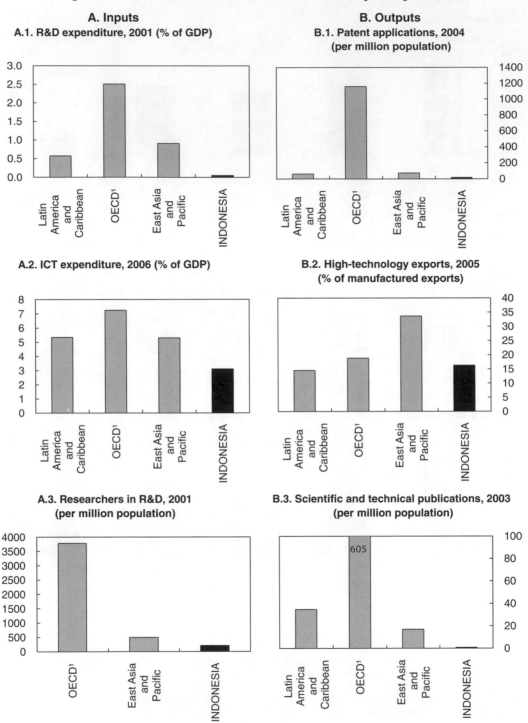

A. Inputs
A.1. R&D expenditure, 2001 (% of GDP)

A.2. ICT expenditure, 2006 (% of GDP)

A.3. Researchers in R&D, 2001
(per million population)

B. Outputs
B.1. Patent applications, 2004
(per million population)

B.2. High-technology exports, 2005
(% of manufactured exports)

B.3. Scientific and technical publications, 2003
(per million population)

StatLink http://dx.doi.org/10.1787/414776662653

1. Excludes Czech Republic, Hungary, Korea, Mexico, Slovak Republic and Turkey.

Source: World Bank (*World Development Indicators*).

Policy considerations

Policy efforts to boost human capital accumulation and innovation should focus not only on increasing educational attainment, especially at the upper secondary and tertiary levels, but also on improving performance. To some extent, the planned increase in budgetary appropriations to meet the requirement that at least 20% of government spending should be allocated to education would go some way in financing the attendant costs. But this requirement raises the question of whether or not this spending level is attainable in the near term, especially if teachers' compensation, which accounts for the lion's share of spending, is excluded from the mandated floor. The realism and desirability of the 20% spending target would therefore need to be carefully assessed. At a minimum, the floor should be redefined to include expenditure on personnel, which was excluded from 2003. In any case, it is unclear whether a rapid increase in budgetary appropriations would deliver a commensurate improvement in outcomes. International experience suggests that, for increases in outlays to bear fruit, they need to be accompanied by complementary policies to improve the efficiency of spending, including teacher training.

But initiatives to improve formal education will not benefit those workers who are already in the labour force. Vocational education and training are under the purview of local jurisdictions, although the central government retains a coordinating and supervisory role. There is little information on the programmes currently in place, especially those provided by private institutions, which are also active in this area. It is nevertheless clear that opportunities for labour training are scarce, even for formal-sector workers, and non-existent for those outside the formal labour market. The 2003 Manpower Law, discussed in detail in Chapter 3, calls for the creation of a national vocational training system. Effort should therefore be focused on putting in place affordable, cost-effective programmes for labour training that could also be extended to informal-sector workers.

Skills certification should be expanded. The 2003 Manpower Law also covers this area, which is carried out by institutions accredited by the government. The move as from 2003 towards competency-based, rather than training-oriented, certification is welcome. But the number of competencies for which certification is currently available is limited. There is also considerable fragmentation in the system, with several competencies applying to a single occupation. Therefore, it would be desirable to expand the certification system to cover more occupations, especially those in the most dynamic sectors of the economy, and to develop cross-competency certifications that would provide a better match between occupations and their required competencies. Greater effort in this area could go in the direction of upskilling the labour force and equipping workers, especially those with informal-sector occupations, with marketable competencies. This is important, because the empirical evidence reported in Chapter 3 shows that educational attainment is a very powerful predictor of a worker's employability in the formal sector.

The performance of Indonesian students suggests that there is ample room for improvement. The authorities are well aware of the need to make steady progress in this area and have begun to take action. There is fairly broad agreement, based on international experience, that the quality of teachers is an important determinant of student performance. To tackle deficiencies in this area, a law on skills certification for teachers was enacted in 2005 (World Bank, 2007; Arze del Granado et al., 2007). Of course, for these efforts to come to fruition, follow-through is essential, and the capacity of local governments – which have become the main providers of educational services since decentralisation in 2001 – to ensure high standards will need to be enhanced and monitored carefully. Should teachers' compensation be included in the minimum spending floor for education, additional funds would have to be made available for financing training programmes for teachers.

In countries with comparatively low innovation intensity, foreign direct investment and imports of capital goods and intermediate inputs are important conduits for technological progress. Further reductions of tariff protection for such goods would therefore be welcome and could facilitate access by Indonesian firms to new technologies embodied in imported inputs, machinery and raw materials. But it should also be recognised that the scope for technological spillovers between foreign affiliates and local companies tends to be reduced when the technological gap between these firms is too large (de Mello, 1999; Takii, 2005). This suggests that policy effort to foster innovation in the business sector can go some way in equipping local firms to make the most of foreign investment in terms of technological upgrading.

Making the regulatory framework in product markets more pro-competition

Background

To gauge the extent of restrictions in Indonesia's product-market regulations, a quantitative indicator was constructed based on the methodology used in the OECD *International Regulation Database* to describe the variability of regulatory approaches in the OECD area (Annex 1.A3). The results, reported in Table 1.5, show that Indonesia's score is much higher than the average of OECD countries and slightly above that of the Latin American countries for which information is available (Brazil, Chile and Mexico, which is an OECD member country). This indicates that Indonesia's regulatory framework in product markets is more restrictive than those in the OECD area, Brazil and Chile. But Indonesia fares well in relation to India, the only regional comparator country for which the PMR indicator is currently available, and South Africa.

The assessment of Indonesia's regulatory environment in product markets suggests considerable scope for reform. In particular, with respect to inward-oriented policies, the restrictiveness of Indonesia's regulatory framework is comparable to that of other emerging-market economies in the OECD area. Regulations are nevertheless more restrictive than in Latin America on average but significantly less so than in India. In particular, pro-competition forces are thwarted by interventionism in many areas, in spite of recent deregulation efforts and reform. For example, the Indonesian government owns the largest firms in several sectors (generation/import, transmission and distribution of electricity; production and import of gas; water production and distribution; and postal services) and is the majority owner of the largest firm in other sectors, including transmission and distribution of gas, and telecommunications. The government also has a stake in some manufacturing sectors and insurance. With regards to barriers to entrepreneurship, administrative burdens are comparatively light in relation to comparator countries in the OECD area and Latin America, although some sector-specific restrictions remain, including in transport and retail distribution.

With regard to outward-oriented policies, the restrictiveness of Indonesia's regulatory framework is on a par with those of other emerging-market economies in the OECD area. It is nevertheless less restrictive than in Latin America and especially India. Ownership and regulatory barriers to foreign investment remain; they are comparable to those of

Table 1.5. **Product market regulations: Cross-country comparisons**

Low scores indicate less restriction[1]

	Indonesia	India	South Africa	Latin America	OECD emerging markets	OECD
Product market regulation	2.1	2.9	2.6	2.0	2.0	1.5
Inward-oriented policies	2.2	3.0	2.7	1.9	2.2	1.8
State control	3.3	3.5	3.2	2.1	2.5	2.1
1. Public ownership	3.8	3.8	3.5	1.9	2.7	2.4
Scope of public enterprise sector	5.7	4.9	4.8	3.0	3.8	3.1
Size of public enterprise sector	4.6	4.6	4.2	1.4	2.4	2.5
Direct control over business enterprises	1.9	2.5	2.3	2.0	2.1	1.9
2. Involvement in business operation	2.7	3.0	2.7	2.3	2.2	1.7
Use of command and control regulation	4.6	5.0	3.2	3.2	2.8	2.2
Price controls	0.5	0.8	2.0	1.3	1.5	1.0
Barriers to entrepreneurship	1.2	2.6	2.2	1.8	2.0	1.5
1. Regulatory and administrative opacity	0.4	1.6	3.5	1.7	1.6	1.4
Licence and permits system	0.0	1.8	6.0	2.0	2.3	2.2
Communication and simplification of rules and procedures	0.6	0.9	0.9	1.3	0.5	0.5
2. Administrative burdens on start-ups	1.7	3.8	1.4	2.1	2.7	1.8
Administrative burdens for corporation	1.0	4.3	1.8	1.8	2.9	1.9
Administrative burdens for sole proprietor firms	2.3	4.8	1.3	3.1	2.8	1.9
Sector specific administrative burdens	1.7	3.3	0.8	1.6	2.7	1.6
3. Barriers to competition	1.1	1.2	2.2	1.2	1.0	0.8
Legal barriers	4.0	0.9	2.2	2.0	1.2	1.4
Antitrust exemptions	0.0	1.2	2.2	0.9	0.9	0.4
Outward-oriented policies	1.8	2.6	2.4	2.2	1.7	1.1
Barriers to trade and investment	1.7	2.6	2.3	2.2	1.7	1.0
1. Explicit barriers	2.0	3.0	2.3	2.2	2.4	1.4
Ownership barriers	3.0	2.9	2.3	1.6	2.6	1.8
Discriminatory procedures	0.0	2.0	2.7	1.4	0.7	0.5
Tariffs	2.0	4.0	2.0	3.7	3.3	1.4
2. Other barriers	1.5	2.0	2.4	2.2	0.8	0.5
Regulatory barriers	1.6	1.6	2.4	2.2	0.3	0.2
Memorandum items:						
Policies by functional area						
Administrative regulation	1.1	3.0	2.2	1.9	2.3	1.6
1. Administrative burdens of start-ups	1.6	4.0	1.3	2.1	2.7	1.8
2. Regulatory and administrative opacity	0.4	1.5	3.4	1.7	1.5	1.4
Economic regulation	2.9	2.7	2.9	1.9	2.1	1.8
1. Regulation of economic structure	4.1	3.0	3.3	2.1	2.3	2.2
2. Regulation of economic behaviour	2.9	3.3	2.8	2.3	2.4	1.9
3. Regulation of competition	0.9	1.4	2.3	1.2	1.3	0.9

1. The scores refer to the status of regulations in 2003 for the OECD countries and Chile, 2004 for Brazil and 2007 for Indonesia and South Africa. Latin America includes Brazil, Chile and Mexico. OECD emerging markets include Czech Republic, Hungary, Korea, Mexico, Poland, Slovak Republic and Turkey.

Source: OECD (2003, 2004, 2007 and 2008) and OECD calculations.

Canada, Italy, Mexico and Turkey, where such restrictions are particularly stringent in the OECD area. Foreign ownership restrictions are particularly burdensome in sectors, such as telecommunications, retail distribution and transport. This is despite the considerable improvements brought about by enactment of the Investment Law (discussed in Chapter 2, together with Indonesia's foreign investment regulations on the basis of the OECD methodology for quantifying the restrictiveness of such provisions for its member countries). Regulatory barriers are also particularly burdensome in Indonesia in comparison with OECD countries, but less so than in Latin America.

Policy considerations

Competition is a key driver of productivity growth in OECD countries.[11] Restrictive regulations in product markets have an adverse effect on an economy's growth performance, because they hamper the reallocation of factors of production towards higher-productivity sectors. This is also the case in Indonesia, given the enterprise-level evidence reported above that reallocation effects have been important sources of productivity gains in manufacturing. A removal of restrictions that forestall competition in product markets would therefore probably contribute to productivity enhancement in support of faster growth.

There is considerable room for reducing the size and scope of government so as to make Indonesia's regulatory framework in product markets more pro-competition. Indonesia's efforts to modernise its economy through privatisation in the 1990s, including recent attempts to liberalise State-owned monopolies in key industries, should be praised. But the extent of government ownership in selected sectors, such as network industries, shows that there is much to be done. The experience of several countries in the OECD and Latin America suggests that, where appropriately designed regulatory frameworks are in place, the withdrawal of the State from manufacturing and network industries has been accompanied by an expansion of supply, a reduction in prices and increases in productivity. Against this background, the authorities' privatisation programme should be given utmost support. In addition, the legal barriers that currently exist on the number of competitors in those sectors where the government has majority (or full) ownership should be removed, especially in financial services, public utilities and transport.

At the same time, the regulatory framework could become friendlier to entrepreneurs. Coordination with sub-national governments could be bolstered, given the increased role played by the sub-national jurisdictions in regulatory matters. As discussed in Chapter 2, at a minimum, a programme could be set up at the national level to review and reduce the number of licenses and permits issued by the local jurisdictions. Effort should also be stepped up to remove remaining ownership barriers to foreign investment. This is important for boosting the economy's growth potential not only through alternative financing for much needed investment in physical capital, but also to encourage productivity enhancement through competition and access to technology.

Tackling infrastructure bottlenecks

Background

Despite a recovery in investment flows in recent years, Indonesia's investment-to-GDP ratio is lower than in many regional comparator countries (Figure 1.10). Unlike public investment, which has risen to its pre-crisis level, private investment has yet to recover fully. It is true that investment ratios were higher in most regional peers before the financial crisis, reflecting to a large extent inefficient capital accumulation during most of the 1990s. The stock of FDI is also relatively low in relation to GDP in Indonesia and has not yet recovered to its pre-crisis level. To the extent that FDI is an important source of finance for investment and a conduit for technological progress, low FDI-to-GDP ratios may be a source of concern.

Figure 1.10. **Investment and FDI: Trends and cross-country comparisons**

A. Investment trends, 1980-2007

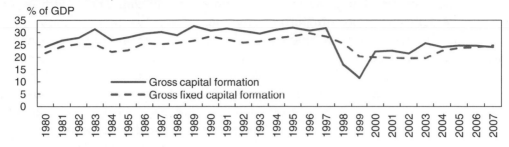

B. Investment-to-GDP ratios, 2006

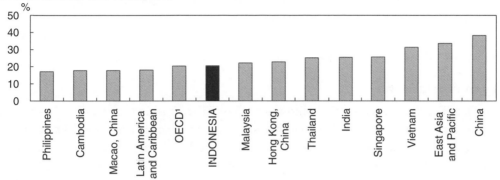

C. FDI stock-to-GDP ratios, 2006

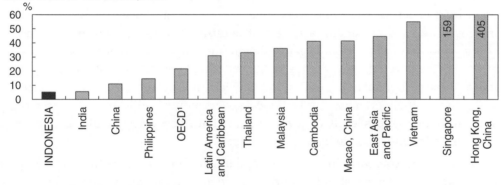

D. FDI net inflows and stocks, 1980-2006

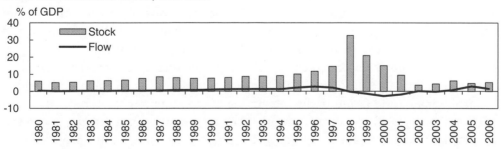

StatLink ⧉ http://dx.doi.org/10.1787/414786450013

1. Excludes Hungary, Mexico, Poland, Slovak Republic and Turkey.

Source: UNCTAD, World Bank (*World Development Indicators*) and OECD calculations.

Indonesia appears to suffer from a dearth of infrastructure, which is likely to hinder growth. As discussed in Chapter 2, basic infrastructure indicators, especially in energy, transport and water/sanitation are particularly poor, even in comparison with regional peers. These deficiencies pose important obstacles to improvements in the country's investment climate. There are therefore reasons to expect higher investment in infrastructure development to be growth-enhancing in the short term. More generally, there is fairly general agreement that the link between infrastructure and growth tends to be stronger in lower-income countries, where infrastructure deficiencies are most pressing.[12] Empirical evidence also suggests that this relationship changes over time, often in a non-linear fashion, because overall economic conditions and regulations are expected to affect firms' abilities to take advantage of infrastructure development and the associated network externalities.[13] Moreover, because there are complementarities between infrastructure development and investment in human and physical capital, infrastructure is likely to raise the productivity of investment in other types of capital, even when its own direct impact on growth is diminishing.[14]

Policy considerations

It is difficult to estimate the amount of investment needed to bolster infrastructure development. For example, for lower-middle income countries, such as Indonesia, investment needs have been estimated for the period 2005-15 at nearly 6.5% of GDP per year on average, including 2.5% of GDP in maintenance (Fay and Yepes, 2003).[15] More important than the magnitude of these estimates is the recognition that there are trade-offs that need to be taken into account in the allocation of scarce budgetary resources between infrastructure and non-infrastructure investment. Measures of social rates of return could be used as benchmarks, but it is difficult to calculate them reliably. It is therefore important to find ways to gauge the productivity of different types of investment in infrastructure development relative to that of other types of capital, including human capital, and the complementarities that might exist among these investments. In any case, given the increasingly prominent role of local governments in this area, it is important to boost coordination across levels of government in both policy design and service delivery and to improve technical capacity at the local level.

Bearing these tradeoffs in mind, it appears that efforts to reduce transport and communication bottlenecks should feature prominently in the infrastructure development agenda of archipelago nations, such as Indonesia. On the basis of the estimates reported for Indonesia by Canning and Bennathan (2000), the social rate of return to investment in transport (paved roads) far outweighs that of investment in electricity generation and in other types of physical capital accumulation. There are numerous efficiency gains that are expected to emerge from progress in this area. For example, better transport and communication infrastructure would likely have spillover effects on trade, both regionally and internationally, and facilitate the integration of the more remote parts of the country into national and global economic networks. The attendant impact on supply conditions should not be underestimated, especially if supported by concomitant pro-competition initiatives in product and labour markets. This is also important for the conduct of monetary policy, because supply-related factors are believed to account for some of the downward price rigidity that has maintained Indonesia's inflation above that of its trading partners.

In addition to economic efficiency considerations, better infrastructure can also affect the living conditions of the poor, to the extent that they are granted access to affordable services. The payoff of policy action in this area is manifold. For example, by reducing distances and travel costs, improvements in transport infrastructure are likely to raise the value of the assets of the poor, especially those living in remote areas, and to reduce their production costs, such as those related to the shipping of agricultural produce to consumer markets. In addition, better transport infrastructure and connection to the electricity grid facilitate access to schools, which fosters human capital accumulation and subsequently improves the earnings potential of the low-income population. Moreover, water and sanitation infrastructure reduces the risk of water-borne diseases and therefore boosts the health status of the poor, which is known to be closely associated with their earnings capabilities.

Access considerations also often depend on affordability, rather than simply physical connectivity to services. Ill-designed, poorly targeted subsidies would make services affordable but at the cost of diverting budgetary resources to the non-poor, while at the same time distorting relative prices (discussed above and in Chapter 3 and OECD, 2002b). These are complex policy issues, but efforts to replace price subsidies for electricity and fuels by targeted transfers to low-income individuals would go in the right direction. In addition, affordability can be improved through sectoral regulations that boost competition in service delivery and therefore contribute to lowering service costs. The removal of constraints on private-sector involvement in network industries, which pose considerable obstacles in some sectors on the basis of the analysis of restrictions in product-market regulations, could be considered as a policy option to enhance competition in product markets.

Making the labour code more flexible

Background

Indonesia's labour code is characterised by burdensome dismissal procedures and severance compensation entitlements in relation to several countries in the OECD area and regional peers. It has also become more restrictive over time, especially after enactment of the Manpower Law of 2003. Minimum-wage provisions have also become increasingly onerous, especially since decentralisation in 2001, when local governments have been granted additional prerogatives in this area. As discussed in Chapter 3, the restrictive labour code is detrimental to growth, because it perpetuates segmentation in the labour market in a country where informality is already widespread. It also has an adverse effect on trade competitiveness, given Indonesia's comparative advantage in the production of labour-intensive goods. Enterprises are likely to have substituted skilled labour and capital for unskilled labour in response to the higher costs associated with a progressively more onerous labour legislation.

The discussion in Chapter 3 also shows that restrictive employment protection legislation is inequitable. It protects workers who are typically better educated and more able to fend for themselves against adverse economic shocks, to the detriment of those in the informal sector and with the most tenuous attachment to the formal labour market, such as women and youths. Therefore, in addition to taking a toll on economic efficiency, a strict labour code fails to provide social protection for those workers who would be most vulnerable to changing labour-market conditions.

Policy considerations

To the extent that burdensome labour laws penalise vulnerable workers instead of protecting them, their use as a social protection device should be called into question. Policy action should therefore be focused on making the labour legislation more flexible for both regular and temporary/fixed-term contracts. The review of the 2003 Manpower Law – which was planned for 2005-06 but did not come to fruition – would provide an invaluable opportunity for making progress in this important policy area. Several options are proposed in Chapter 3 for achieving this goal, while bearing in mind the need to strengthen Indonesia's safety nets in a fiscally sound manner and to deal with the trade-offs associated with the allocation of scarce budgetary resources to satisfy competing demands for human capital accumulation, social protection and infrastructure development. The authorities' efforts in this area since the 1997-98 crisis through community-based and targeted income transfers to vulnerable and poor individuals are commendable. Additional policy options for further improvement in this area are also discussed below.

Notes

1. See Hill (2007) and Hill and Shiraishi (2007) for more information.

2. See Athukorala (2006) for more information. The share of electronics goods (parts and components) in Indonesia's exports is about 9%, against 21% and 36% in Thailand and Malaysia, respectively. Indonesia has also under-performed in major export destinations, notably China, Japan and the United States.

3. See Basri and Papanek (2008) for more information.

4. In the case of electronics, Indonesia has begun to develop an export-oriented assembly sector connected to global production networks, although it is still a minor player in the main East Asian networks (Athukorala, 2006).

5. Rice is the main food crop produced, followed by cassava and maize. Non-food crops include rubber, oil palm, coffee, tea, cocoa and sugar cane. Poultry is the fastest growing livestock production.

6. Evidence for the OECD shows that relatively pervasive employment protection and anti-competitive regulations in goods markets tend to curb FDI (Hajkova *et al.*, 2006). In a similar vein, Blomström and Kokko (1993) find that the intensity of the technological transfer from US firms investing abroad increases with competition in the host country.

7. Takii and Ramstetter (2005) highlight a discrepancy in FDI trends calculated on the basis of the balance of payments and *Statistik Industri*. Accordingly, industrial-survey data do not show a fall in foreign ownership in manufacturing, as opposed to the balance-of-payments estimates.

8. The government's original proposal was that taxpayers who wished to appeal against their tax assessment should make an initial payment in advance. If the appeal were rejected, the taxpayer would have to pay a fine of up to 100% of his/her tax liability. Taxpayers could appeal again, but the fine would increase to 200% of tax liabilities for a failed appeal. This proposal was rejected, and the law approved by Parliament in 2007 requires no advance payment for appeals and sets fines at 50% and 100% of tax liabilities, respectively. The new law also provides for punishing tax officials who are found to have treated taxpayers unjustly.

9. Expenditure on both types of subsidy is strongly correlated, because higher oil prices affects the cost of electricity generation, given Indonesia's reliance on diesel-based power plants.

10. See Rosengard (2004) for a detailed analysis of Indonesia's fiscal performance before and after the crisis.

11. See OECD (2002a), for empirical evidence on the linkages between the intensity of competition in product markets and productivity performance.

12. See Estache and Fay (2007) for a survey of the empirical literature.

13. These non-linearities in the relationship between infrastructure investment and growth arise from network effects. See Hurlin (2006) for cross-country evidence for a large number of developing and developed countries with emphasis on roads, railways, telecommunications and electricity.

14. See Canning and Bennathan (2000) for cross-country evidence of the elasticity of output with respect to infrastructure development (measured by paved roads and electricity generation capacity) in the presence of complementarities between different types of capital.

15. The estimates refer to the investment necessary to satisfy consumer and producer demand on the basis of projected GDP growth and include the following sectors: roads, railways, telecommunications, electricity, water and sanitation.

Bibliography

Amiti, M. and J. Konings (2005), "Trade Liberalisation, Intermediate Inputs and Productivity: Evidence from Indonesia", *IMF Working Paper*, No. WP/05/146, International Monetary Fund, Washington, D.C.

Arze del Granado, F.J., W. Fengler, A. Ragatz and E. Yavuz (2007), "Investing in Indonesia's Education: Allocation, Equity and Efficiency of Public Expenditures", *Policy Research Working Paper*, No. 4329, World Bank, Washington, D.C.

Aswicahyono, H. and H. Hill (2002), "'Perspiration' and 'Inspiration' in Asian Industrialisation: Indonesia Before the Crisis", *Journal of Development Studies*, Vol. 38, pp. 138-63.

Athukorala, P.C. (2006), "Post-crisis Export Performance: The Indonesian Experience in Regional Perspective", *Bulletin of Indonesian Economic Studies*, Vol. 42, pp. 177-211.

Basri, M.C. and H. Soesastro (2005), "The Political Economy of Trade Policy in Indonesia", *ASEAN Economic Bulletin*, Vol. 22, pp. 3-18.

Basri, M.C. and G. Papanek (2008), "Dutch Disease and Employment in Indonesia", *Working Paper*, LPEM-FEUI, University of Indonesia, Jakarta.

Blomström, M. and A. Kokko (1993), "Policies to Encourage Inflows of Technology through Foreign Multinationals", *World Development*, Vol. 23, pp. 459-68.

Canning, D. and E. Bennathan (2000), "The Social Rate of Return on Infrastructure Investments", *Policy Research Working Paper*, No. 2390, World Bank, Washington, D.C.

Conway, P., V. Janod and G. Nicoletti (2005), "Product Market Regulations in OECD Countries: 1998 to 2003", *Economics Department Working Paper*, No. 419, OECD, Paris.

de Mello, L. (1999), "Foreign Direct Investment-Led Growth: Evidence from Time Series and Panel Data", *Oxford Economic Papers*, Vol. 51, pp. 133-51.

de Mello, L. (2000), "Fiscal Decentralization and Intergovernmental Fiscal Relations: A Cross-Country Analysis", *World Development*, Vol. 28, pp. 365-80.

Estache, A. and M. Fay (2007), "Current Debates on Infrastructure Policy", *Policy Research Working Paper*, No. 4410, World Bank, Washington, D.C.

Fay, M. and T. Yepes (2003), "Investing in Infrastructure: What is Needed from 2000-2010", *Policy Research Working Paper*, No. 3102, World Bank, Washington, D.C.

Fitrani, F., B. Hofman and K. Kaiser (2005), "Unity or Diversity? The Creation of New Local Governments in a Decentralised Indonesia", *Bulletin of Indonesian Economic Studies*, Vol. 41, pp. 57-79.

Fuglie, K. (2004), "Productivity Growth in Indonesian Agriculture, 1961-2000", *Bulletin of Indonesian Economic Studies*, Vol. 40, pp. 209-25.

Hajkova, D., G. Nicoletti, L. Vartia and K.-Y. Yoo (2006), "Taxation, Business Environment and FDI Location in OECD Countries", *OECD Economics Department Working Paper*, No. 502, OECD, Paris.

Hill, H. (2007), "The Indonesian Economy: Growth, Crisis and Recovery", *Singapore Economic Review*, Vol. 52, pp. 137-66.

Hill, H. and T. Shiraishi (2007), "The Indonesian Economy: A Decade after the Crisis", *Asian Economic Policy Review*, Vol. 2, pp. 127-45.

Hofman, B., K. Kaiser Kadjatmiko and B.S. Sjahrir (2006), "Evaluating Fiscal Equalisation in Indonesia", *World Bank Policy Research Working Paper*, No. 3911, World Bank, Washington, D.C.

Hurlin, C. (2006), "Network Effects of the Productivity of Infrastructure in Developing Countries", *Policy Research Working Paper*, No. 3808, World Bank, Washington, D.C.

Jain-Chandra, S. (2007), "Is Indonesia Adequately Integrated into Global and Regional Trade and Finance?", *Indonesia: Selected Issues*, IMF Country Report No. 07/273, International Monetary Fund, Washington, D.C.

Lewis, B.D. (2006), "Local Government Taxation: An Analysis of Administrative Cost Inefficiency", *Bulletin of Indonesian Economic Studies*, Vol. 42, pp. 213-33.

Narjoko, D. (2006), *Indonesian Manufacturing and the Economic Crisis of 1997/98*, PhD thesis, Australian National University, Canberra.

Nicoletti, G., S. Scarpetta and O. Boylaud (1999), "Summary Indicators of Product Market Regulation with an Extension to Employment Protection Legislation", *Economics Department Working Papers*, No. 226, OECD, Paris.

OECD (2002a), *OECD Economic Outlook*, No. 72, OECD, Paris.

OECD (2002b), *Towards Asia's Sustainable Development: The Role of Social Protection*, OECD, Paris.

OECD (2003), *OECD Economic Survey of Chile*, OECD, Paris.

OECD (2004), *OECD Economic Survey of Brazil*, OECD, Paris.

OECD (2007), *OECD Economic Survey of India*, OECD, Paris.

OECD (2008), *OECD Economic Assessment of South Africa*, OECD, Paris.

Rosengard, J. (2004), "Will Bank Bailouts Bust Budgets? Fiscalisation of the East Asian Financial Crisis", *Asian-Pacific Economic Literature*, Vol. 18, pp. 19-29.

Sarel, M. (1997), "Growth and Productivity in ASEAN Countries", *Working Paper*, No. 97/97, International Monetary Fund, Washington, D.C.

Sarwono, H. (2008), "Monetary Policy in Emerging Markets: The Case of Indonesia", in L. de Mello (ed.), *Inflation Targeting in Emerging-Market Economies*, OECD, Paris.

Sjöholm, F. (1999a), "Exports, Imports and Productivity: Results from Indonesian Establishment Data", *World Development*, Vol. 27, pp. 705-15.

Sjöholm, F. (1999b), "Technology Gap, Competition and Spillovers from Direct Foreign Investment: Evidence from Establishment Data", *Journal of Development Studies*, Vol. 36, pp. 53-73.

Takii, S. (2005), "Productivity Spillovers and Characteristics of Foreign Multinational Plants in Indonesian Manufacturing 1990-95", *Journal of Development Economics*, Vol. 76, pp. 521-42.

Takii, S. and E.D. Ramstetter (2005), "Multinational Presence and Labour Productivity Differentials in Indonesian Manufacturing, 1975-2001", *Bulletin of Indonesian Economic Studies*, Vol. 41, pp. 221-42.

Ter Wengel, J. and E.R. Rodriguez (2006), "Productivity and Firm Dynamics; Creative Destruction in Indonesian Manufacturing, 1994-2000", *Bulletin of Indonesian Economic Studies*, Vol. 42, pp. 341-55.

Timmer, M.P. (1999), "Indonesia's Ascent on the Technology Ladder: Capital Stock and Total Factor Productivity in Indonesian Manufacturing, 1975-95", *Bulletin of Indonesian Economic Studies*, Vol. 35, pp. 75-97.

Van der Eng, P. (2007), "Total Factor Productivity and Economic Growth in Indonesia", unpublished manuscript, School of Management, Marketing and International Business, Australian National University, Canberra.

Vial, V. (2006), "New Estimates of Total Factor Productivity Growth in Indonesian Manufacturing", *Bulletin of Indonesian Economic Studies*, Vol. 42, pp. 357-69.

Warr, P. (2006), "Productivity Growth in Thailand and Indonesia: How Agriculture Contributes to Economic Growth", *Working Paper in Economics and Development Studies*, No. 200606, Department of Economics, Padjadjaran University, Bandung.

World Bank (2006), "Revitalizing the Rural Economy: An Assessment of the Investment Climate Faced by Non-Farm Enterprises at the District Level", World Bank, Washington, D.C.

World Bank (2007), *Indonesia Public Expenditure Review 2007*, World Bank, Washington, D.C.

ANNEX 1.A1

Estimating Indonesia's potential GDP

This Annex calculates trend GDP for five Asian countries that were affected by the financial crisis of 1997-98 (Indonesia, Korea, Malaysia, Philippines and Thailand) using a production function approach akin to that used by the OECD Secretariat for its member countries.

Methodology

As a first step, total factor productivity was calculated as follows:

$$\ln(TFP_t) = \ln(Y_t) - r_K \ln(\overline{K}_t) - r_L \ln(\overline{L}_t),$$
(1.A1.1)

where Y_t denotes real GDP; $\overline{K}_t = \gamma_t K_t$ is the utilisation-adjusted capital stock, where $\gamma_t = (1 - u_t)$ denotes a coefficient of utilisation of installed capacity, u_t is the rate of unemployment, and K_t is the capital stock; $\overline{L}_t = (1 - u_t)\overline{F}_t$ is utilisation-adjusted labour, where $\overline{F}_t$ denotes the labour force; ln(.) denotes the natural logarithm; and t is a time indicator. The shares of capital and labour in GDP (r_k and r_L, respectively) are set at 33 and 67%, respectively.[1]

Finally, trend GDP was calculated as follows:

$$\ln(Y_t^*) = \ln(TFP_t)^* + 0.33 \ln(K_t^*) + 0.67 \ln(L_t^*),$$
(1.A1.2)

where the asterisks indicate that the series are HP-filtered. Forecasts of the relevant series using an AR model were estimated for 2007-10 (2008-10 for Indonesia) and used to compute the HP trends in order to minimise the end-point bias associated with HP filtering.[2]

Data

To ensure cross-country comparability, annual data available from the IMF's *International Financial Statistics* (IFS) database were used in the calculations for the period 1980-2006 for all countries (data from national sources were used to update the series for Indonesia through 2007). The variables of interest are: GDP, gross capital formation, labour force and the unemployment rate. The GDP and gross capital formation series are in constant USD using 2000 PPP parities. The capital stocks were constructed using the perpetual inventory method (for investment series starting in 1960 and using a fixed depreciation rate of 5%). Missing values in the unemployment series were interpolated linearly and updated from national sources.

Findings

Based on the methodology above, total factor productivity growth appears to be bouncing back in all countries, especially Indonesia and Thailand (Figure 1.A1.1). TFP growth has contributed about 1.5 percentage points to Indonesia's trend GDP growth per year on average since 2000. Based on the growth-accounting exercise, trend GDP growth

Figure 1.A1.1. **Trend GDP growth: Cross-country comparisons, 1980-2006**[1]

In per cent

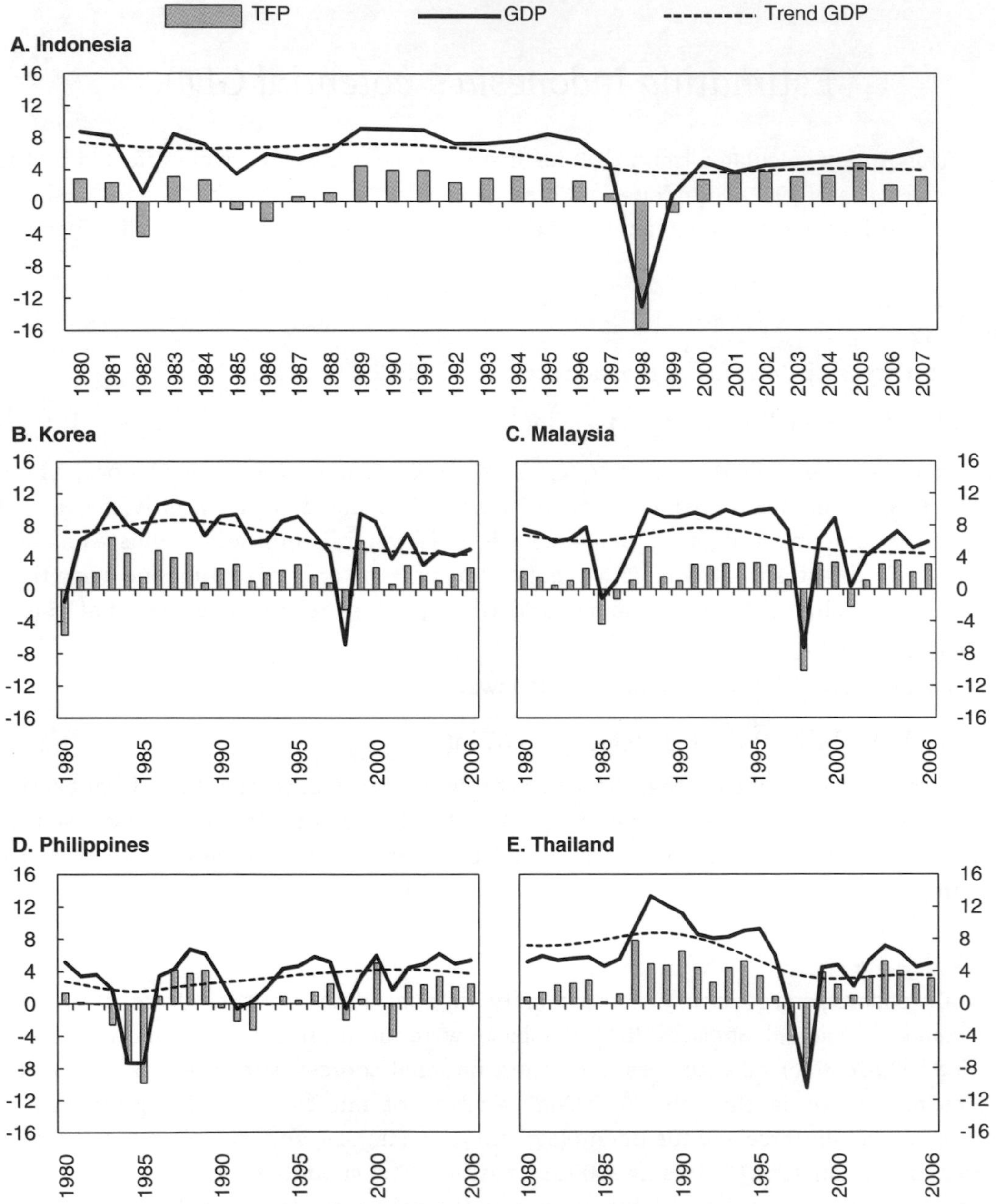

StatLink http://dx.doi.org/10.1787/414825647612

1. 1980-2007 for Indonesia.

Source: World Bank (World Development Indicators) and OECD calculations.

seems to be in the neighbourhood of 4% per year in Indonesia, still below the average of the pre-crisis period (1990-96) of about 6%. Indonesia's trend growth rate is estimated to be slightly lower than those of Korea and Malaysia, but higher than those of Thailand and the Philippines.[3]

Important caveats

The calculations reported above should be interpreted with caution, because growth accounting has obvious limitations, which are well known. In particular:

- The computation of TFP is sensitive to measurement errors, because it is by definition a residual (*i.e.* the difference between output growth and a weighted average of the growth rates of the utilisation-adjusted factors of production). TFP estimates are also sensitive to the measurement of capital and labour shares in national income. A correction is made in the calculations for factor utilisation, because estimates of TFP growth would be pro-cyclical, if the underutilisation of inputs during cyclical downturns were not taken into account. The use of the unemployment rate as a proxy for capital utilisation is obviously imperfect, but unavoidable due to data constraints. Moreover, factor quality is treated in the calculations as constant over time, whereas increases in the stock of human capital of the labour force are expected to affect the economy's overall efficiency.

- Likewise, estimates of trend GDP growth on the basis of growth-accounting exercises are affected by the business cycle. Also, and perhaps most importantly, the effects of ongoing structural reform on efficiency and input accumulation, which take time to come to fruition, are not taken into account in the computation of current trend growth rates using growth accounting.

Notes

1. The capital share used in the exercise is a rough average of those estimated by Sarel (1997) for the ASEAN countries, which are in the range of 28-35%. The ratios implied by the national accounts are implausibly low for these countries, as discussed in the main text.

2. Ideally, the NAICU and NAIRU rates should be used in the calculation of the utilisation-adjusted capital and labour inputs needed to compute trend GDP. However, these series could not be reliably estimated for the countries in the sample due to structural breaks in the relevant series, notably those associated with the financial crisis.

3. Calculations of trend GDP and TFP growth for Korea may differ slightly from those reported in the OECD *Economic Outlook* database because of differences in methodology and data sources. The calculations for Korea were carried out to ensure consistency with the growth-accounting exercises reported for the other countries under consideration.

ANNEX 1.A2

Gauging Indonesia's regional diversity

This Annex provides an overview of the regional distribution of economic activity in Indonesia.* It is not possible to discuss trends at the local government level, since the data series available span a shorter time period.

It is customary to divide Indonesia into five major island groupings: Java-Bali, Sumatra, Kalimantan (Borneo), Sulawesi, and the Eastern provinces (Figure 1.A2.1). Java dominates the economy, accounting for almost two-thirds of GDP and household expenditure (Table 1.A2.1). Sumatra comes next, followed by Kalimantan. Mining, especially oil and gas, inflates the economic activity indicators of the resource-rich provinces: Riau, East Kalimantan, Papua (Irian) and Aceh. Over time, and regardless of the measure used, there has been a shift of economic activity towards Java-Bali, especially Jakarta. Sumatra's share of economic activity has been affected by a falling share of oil and gas in the national economy. At the same time, the share of the eight Eastern provinces in the national economy has been declining. Moreover, there are large inter-provincial differences in income and welfare. The gap in income and consumption per capita between the richest and poorest provinces is very large (Table 1.A2.2). Output per capita in East Kalimantan, the richest province, is nearly 16 times higher than in Maluku.

A few stylised facts emerge from these comparisons. *First*, there is no case of a province with consistently poor performance for sustained periods of time. Even the provinces that have slipped behind have still grown quite strongly since the 1970s, except for the crisis period. *Second*, while there have been consistent good performers, notably Bali, East Kalimantan and Jakarta, the group of top performers has been quite diverse in terms of location, size and socio-economic characteristics. *Third*, economic activity has continued to cluster around some key regional economies, including Java, Bali, Sumatra and Kalimantan, as opposed to the Eastern provinces. *Fifth*, there is no generalised natural-resource pattern: in some cases, resource-rich regions have been associated with uneven development, as in Aceh and, to some extent, Papua. In other cases, for example Riau and East Kalimantan, the abundance of natural resources has been reasonably widely distributed. The provinces that are rich in natural resources have nevertheless benefited from the ongoing commodity-price boom.

---

* Adjustments have been made to pre-2000 data to account for the creation of provinces since 2000. For example, West Java refers to the current provinces of West Java and Banten.

Figure 1.A2.1. **Map of Indonesia**

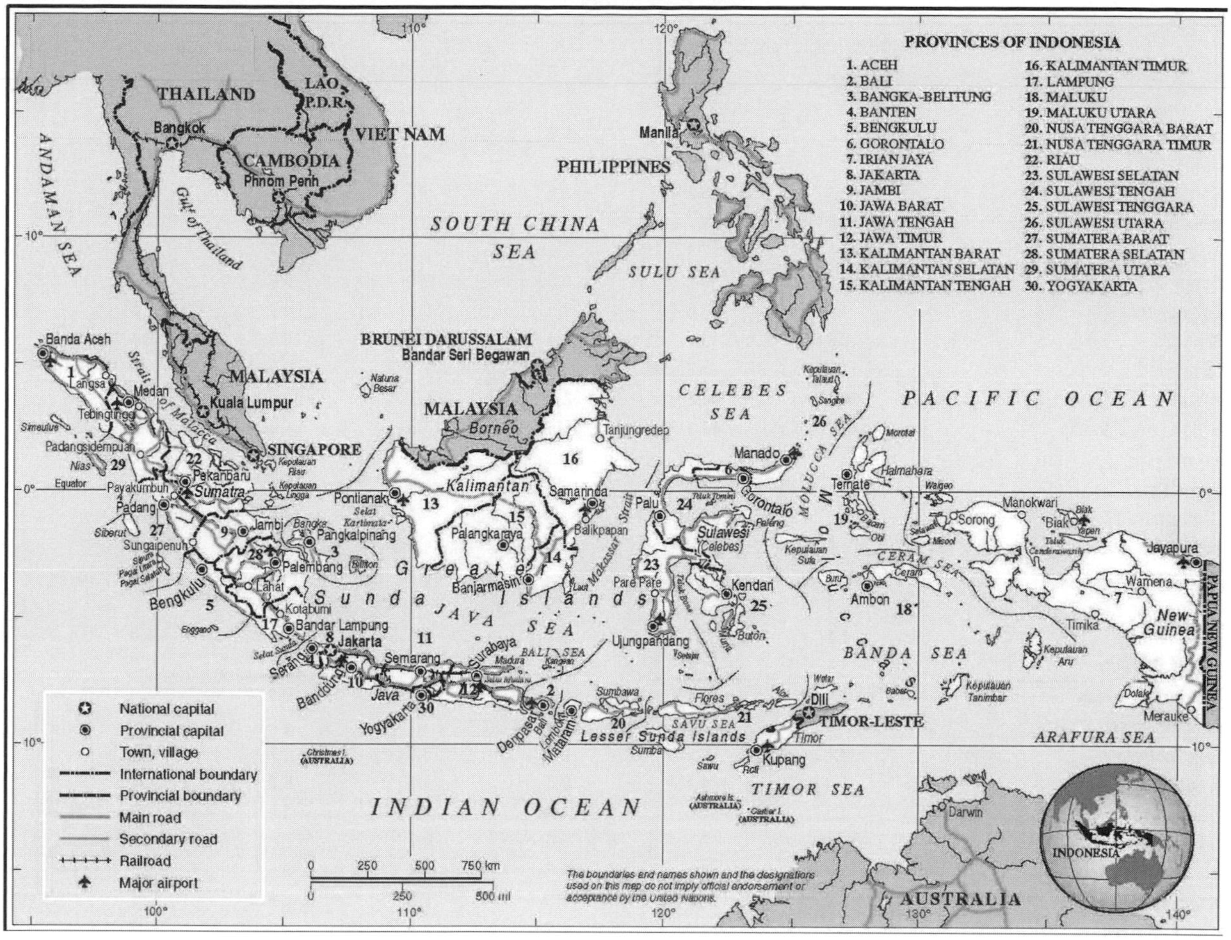

Source: United Nations.

Table 1.A2.1. **Provincial economic activity indicators, 1975-2007**

In per cent of total

	Gross regional product (GRP)		Non-mining GRP		Consumption	
	1975	2007	1975	2007	1983	2004
Sumatra	**32.2**	**23.0**	**21.0**	**20.4**	**20.6**	**20.2**
Aceh	1.6	2.1	1.7	1.6	2.1	0.9
North Sumatra	5.7	5.2	6.6	5.7	6.4	5.4
West Sumatra	1.8	1.7	2.3	1.9	2.2	1.8
Riau	15.1	7.4	2.1	5.2	1.9	5.5
Jambi	0.8	0.9	0.9	0.8	0.6	0.9
South Sumatra	4.8	3.6	4.5	2.9	4.7	3.6
Bengkulu	0.3	0.4	0.4	0.4	0.5	0.4
Lampung	1.9	1.8	2.4	1.9	2.2	1.6
Java-Bali	**51.5**	**60.2**	**62.8**	**64.7**	**64.4**	**67.4**
Java-Bali (w/o Jakarta)	**42.8**	**44.1**	**51.8**	**47.0**	**54.0**	**51.0**
Jakarta	8.7	16.1	11.0	17.8	10.4	16.5
West Java	14.5	18.0	16.3	19.3	17.2	19.0
Central Java	9.9	8.8	12.5	8.5	14.5	10.4
Yogyakarta	1.2	0.9	1.5	1.0	1.6	0.9
East Java	15.8	15.2	19.9	16.8	18.7	19.3
Bali	1.3	1.2	1.6	1.3	2.0	1.3
Kalimantan	**7.1**	**9.1**	**6.1**	**6.4**	**5.4**	**4.6**
West Kalimantan	1.4	1.2	1.8	1.3	1.7	1.3
Central Kalimantan	0.5	0.8	0.7	0.9	0.9	0.9
South Kalimantan	1.0	1.1	1.3	1.2	1.5	0.9
East Kalimantan	4.1	6.0	2.3	3.0	1.2	1.6
Sulawesi	**5.0**	**4.1**	**6.3**	**4.5**	**6.2**	**4.4**
North Sulawesi	1.3	0.8	1.6	0.9	1.3	0.7
Central Sulawesi	0.4	0.6	0.6	0.7	0.8	0.8
South Sulawesi	3.0	2.1	3.8	2.4	3.5	2.4
Southeast Sulawesi	0.3	0.5	0.3	0.6	0.6	0.5
Eastern provinces	**4.3**	**3.6**	**4.0**	**3.9**	**3.5**	**3.3**
West Nusa Tenggara	0.8	1.0	1.0	1.1	1.0	0.7
East Nusa Tenggara	0.8	0.5	1.0	0.6	1.0	0.7
Maluku	0.9	0.3	1.1	0.3	0.9	0.4
Papua	1.8	1.9	0.9	2.0	0.7	1.5

Source: BPS (*Regional Income by Industry and Expenditure*).

OECD ECONOMIC SURVEYS: INDONESIA: ECONOMIC ASSESMENT – ISBN 978-92-64-04805-8 – © OECD 2008

Table 1.A2.2. **Provincial development indicators, 1975-2007**

Indonesia = 100

	GRP per capita		Non-mining GRP per capita		Consumption per capita	
	1975	2007	1975	2007	1983	2004
Sumatra	**177.0**	**108.2**	**115.3**	**96.1**	**104.8**	**93.9**
Aceh	93.3	111.9	97.9	88.1	114.4	49.5
North Sumatra	101.9	90.6	116.7	99.9	111.0	92.3
West Sumatra	79.1	81.4	99.2	90.5	96.8	87.6
Riau	1061.5	259.3	150.2	181.0	128.8	198.0
Jambi	87.1	74.8	101.5	67.9	62.0	75.9
South Sumatra	160.6	100.6	150.1	80.8	144.8	100.5
Bengkulu	61.9	50.4	77.6	56.0	90.5	56.3
Lampung	72.9	54.2	91.6	58.9	62.2	48.4
Java-Bali	**79.4**	**100.6**	**96.9**	**108.2**	**101.9**	**114.2**
Java-Bali (w/o Jakarta)	**70.5**	**79.0**	**85.4**	**84.2**	**92.2**	**92.7**
Jakarta	212.1	400.0	267.1	442.5	224.9	403.0
West Java	78.7	81.7	88.6	87.4	91.3	94.8
Central Java	55.6	61.4	69.6	59.5	85.9	69.4
Yogyakarta	61.6	61.1	77.4	68.0	88.1	59.7
East Java	76.3	92.7	95.9	102.8	96.7	115.2
Bali	77.6	77.8	97.1	86.5	119.0	82.5
Kalimantan	**159.2**	**163.1**	**136.6**	**114.3**	**114.7**	**79.2**
West Kalimantan	84.2	65.0	105.9	72.3	101.9	62.2
Central Kalimantan	88.3	88.1	110.9	97.9	132.7	86.7
South Kalimantan	72.2	74.3	90.5	81.2	110.6	59.3
East Kalimantan	576.5	448.6	325.9	220.5	131.5	123.3
Sulawesi	**70.6**	**56.2**	**87.7**	**62.2**	**87.4**	**59.0**
North Sulawesi	86.9	57.3	109.0	63.7	89.6	51.9
Central Sulawesi	55.1	58.1	69.1	63.2	91.4	67.5
South Sulawesi	70.7	55.4	89.0	61.4	85.7	61.4
Southeast Sulawesi	52.7	56.1	52.8	62.4	87.6	49.8
Eastern provinces	**78.1**	**59.5**	**72.5**	**64.6**	**64.1**	**54.3**
West Nusa Tenggara	45.5	50.5	56.6	56.1	53.9	35.8
East Nusa Tenggara	41.5	27.5	52.1	30.6	52.0	38.5
Maluku	91.9	25.2	113.1	28.0	89.6	38.5
Papua	226.8	154.0	111.1	163.5	84.3	126.2

Source: BPS (Regional Income by Industry and Expenditure).

ANNEX 1.A3

Assessing the restrictiveness of Product Market Regulations

This Annex quantifies the restrictiveness of Indonesia's product market regulations (PMR) on the basis of the OECD methodology (Nicoletti *et al.*, 1999; Conway *et al.*, 2005). The results are reported in the main text.

Methodology

The PMR indicator system has a pyramidal shape, with 16 low-level indicators at the base and one overall indicator of product market regulation at the top. The low-level indicators capture a specific aspect of the regulatory regime summarising information on 137 economy-wide or industry-specific regulatory provisions, based on answers to the OECD Regulatory Indicator questionnaire. Higher-level indicators are constructed as weighted averages of their constituent lower-level indicators. The PMR index ranges between 0 and 6, with 0 indicating the lowest and 6 the highest level of rigidity.

The PMR indicator can be decomposed into two main groups: i) inward-oriented policies, comprising state control and barriers to entrepreneurship, and administrative and economic regulation, and ii) outward-oriented policies corresponding to barriers to trade and investment. The 16 low-level indicators, which cover a wide range of product market policies, are as follows:

- **Scope of public enterprises:** measures the pervasiveness of state ownership across business sectors as the proportion of sectors in which the state has an equity stake in at least one firm.

- **Size of public enterprise:** reflects the overall size of state-owned enterprises relative to the size of the economy.

- **Direct control over business enterprises:** measures the existence of government special voting rights in privately-owned firms, constraints on the sale of state-owned equity stakes, and the extent to which legislative bodies control the strategic choices of public enterprises.

- **Price controls**: reflects the extent of price controls in specific sectors.

- **Use of command and control regulation:** indicates the extent to which government uses coercive (as opposed to incentive-based) regulation in general and in specific service sectors.

- **Licenses and permits systems:** reflects the use of 'one-stop shops' and 'silence is consent' rules for getting information on and issuing licenses and permits.

- **Communication and simplification of rules and procedures:** reflects aspects of government's communication strategy and efforts to reduce and simplify the administrative burden of interacting with government.

- **Administrative burdens for corporations:** measures the administrative burdens on the creation of corporations.

- **Administrative burdens for sole proprietors:** measures the administrative burdens on the creation of sole-proprietor firms.

- **Sector-specific administrative burdens:** reflects administrative burdens in the road transport and retail-distribution sectors.

- **Legal barriers:** measures the scope of explicit legal limitations on the number of competitors allowed in a wide range of business sectors.

- **Antitrust exemptions:** measures the scope of exemptions to competition law for public enterprises.

- **Ownership barriers:** reflects legal restrictions on foreign acquisition of equity generally in public and private firms and specifically in the telecommunications and airlines sectors.

- **Tariffs:** reflects the (simple) average of most-favoured-nation tariffs.

- **Discriminatory procedures:** reflects the extent of discrimination against foreign firms at the procedural level.

- **Regulatory barriers:** reflects other barriers to international trade (*e.g.* international harmonisation, mutual recognition agreements).

The PMR indicators are based primarily on explicit policy settings and account only for formal government regulation. Thus, the indicators record only 'objective' data about rules and regulations, as opposed to 'subjective' assessments of market participants for indicators based on opinion surveys.

ISBN 978-92-64-04805-8
OECD Economic Surveys: Indonesia: Economic Assesment
© OECD 2008

Chapter 2

Improving the business and investment climate

Indonesia's business environment is discouraging entrepreneurship and holding back private-sector growth and development. Weaknesses in the regulatory framework, infrastructure bottlenecks and poor governance continue to weigh down on investment. Policies have been put in place to address these problems, but much remains to be done. An important recent initiative is the enactment of the Investment Law in 2007, which strengthened the foreign investment regime.

This chapter argues that options for reform could focus on making regulations more pro-business, including by removing red tape and onerous provisions at the local level of government, improving governance and relaxing remaining restrictions on foreign investment. Further financial deepening would facilitate access by enterprises to more abundant, cheaper sources of finance.

Indonesia needs to encourage entrepreneurship to boost potential GDP growth through the accumulation of physical capital and productivity gains. Infrastructure bottlenecks, regulatory uncertainty and poor governance are among the main obstacles to investment according to business surveys. The financial sector is by far sounder and deeper than it was ten years ago but can be developed further to allow firms easier, less costly access to alternatives sources of finance. A comfortable fiscal position is creating room in the budget for increasing public investment, especially in infrastructure development. The authorities are well aware of the need for resolute action in several policy areas and lave launched policy packages to encourage investment in infrastructure development, to promote financial development and to attract foreign investment, so as to create the necessary conditions for the private sector to play a more active role in the growth process.

This chapter reviews trends in investment since the 1997-98 crisis, assesses the main impediments to entrepreneurship and discusses options for improving the business climate. Special emphasis is placed on the main provisions of the Investment Law enacted in 2007. The chapter's key policy message is that the business climate needs to improve considerably to unleash opportunities for growth.

Trends in investment and an assessment of the business climate

Trends in investment

As discussed in Chapter 1, despite some renewed dynamism in fixed capital formation in recent years, Indonesia's investment-to-GDP ratio has yet to recover to its pre-crisis level and remains below those of comparator countries in the region. This has raised concern among policymakers about the country's ability to lift and maintain potential growth over the longer term and to match the growth rates of the fast-growing economies in Asia, including China and India. Of course, an economy's growth potential depends on factors other than input accumulation, including – most importantly – the efficiency with which inputs are combined to produce output. Indonesia's growth has hitherto been driven predominantly by the accumulation of inputs, suggesting that much can be done to enhance efficiency in support of faster growth, while removing remaining obstacles to capital accumulation and to effective utilisation of labour (discussed in Chapter 3).

Foreign direct investment is an important source of finance for capital accumulation. Net FDI inflows have recovered in recent years, following a sharp reversal in the wake of the financial crisis of 1997-98. Southeast Asia was among the most attractive FDI destinations outside the OECD area in the first half of the 1990s, a situation that changed radically following the financial crisis. Only recently have FDI inflows recovered to their pre-crisis levels in most countries (Figure 2.1). Indonesia was affected particularly adversely, with net FDI outflows during most of the years from 1998 to 2003. This reversal in investors' sentiment reflected a loss of confidence in the economy's growth potential following the crisis, a deterioration of the business environment with a proliferation of new business regulations by local governments after decentralisation in 2001 and more

Figure 2.1. **Net FDI inflows in Southeast Asia, 1990-2006**

In billions of current USD

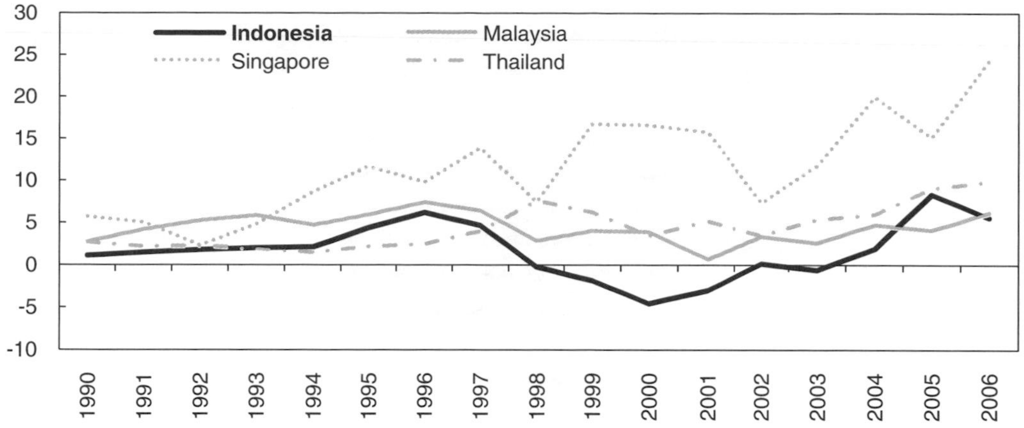

StatLink http://dx.doi.org/10.1787/414831137354

Source: UNCTAD.

burdensome labour regulations with the enactment of a new labour code in 2003 (discussed in Chapter 3).[1]

Investment – both foreign and domestic – is fairly concentrated across sectors, provinces and residency of foreign investors. While domestic investment has focused predominantly on labour-intensive sectors, such as paper, food processing, agriculture and construction, there has been considerable FDI in more capital-intensive activities, such as transport, storage and communications, and in the chemical and pharmaceutical industries. The geographical distribution of investment is also concentrated: foreign investment tends to favour locations in Java (80% of total FDI), whereas domestic firms also invest in Sumatra, which, together with Java, accounts for more than 80% of domestic investment. This pattern isnot surprising, given that these two islands account for a large share of population and economic activity (discussed in Chapter 1). Moreover, the top five foreign investors by country of residency (Singapore, Japan, Chinese Taipei, Korea and Australia) accounted for almost 70% of FDI in the first 10 months of 2007.[2]

Indonesia's business climate

There is considerable consensus among policymakers and the business community that a weak business environment is among the most important obstacles to investment in Indonesia. The main obstacles to entrepreneurship highlighted by the business community in surveys are: macroeconomic instability; regulatory uncertainty, including over taxes and business licensing; deficiencies in law enforcement; instability of contracts; rigidity of labour regulations and poor quality of infrastructure (Figure 2.2). Indonesia also fares poorly in international comparisons, despite an improvement in recent years: according to the FDI Confidence Index surveyed by A.T. Kearney, a management consulting firm, Indonesia ranked 21st among the 25 most attractive FDI destinations in 2007.[3]

Burdensome product market regulations are also detrimental to the business environment. On the basis of the OECD methodology for assessing the restrictiveness of a country's regulatory framework in product markets, discussed in Chapter 1, Indonesia fares particularly poorly in comparison with OECD countries in policy areas related to the

Figure 2.2. **Indonesia's main business constraints, 2003 and 2007**

Per cent of firms reporting the issue as a business constraint[1]

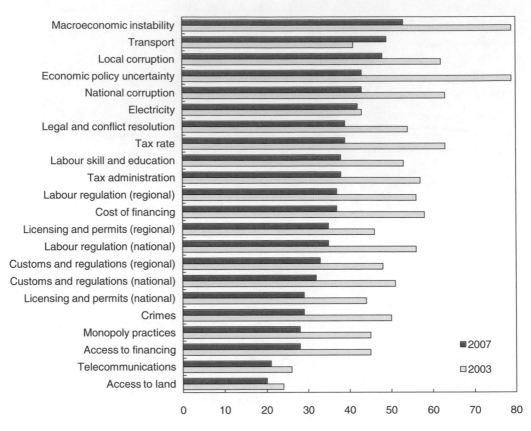

StatLink ᓭᓍᕿ http://dx.doi.org/10.1787/414838075526

1. Data for 2003 is available from Asian Development Bank (2003) and for 2007 from LPEM-FEUI (2007a).

Source: Asian Development Bank (2003) and LPEM-FEUI (2007a).

extent of State control in the economy, given the size and scope of the public-enterprise sector, as well as the use of command-and-control regulations. Remaining restrictions on foreign ownership of domestic firms and a proliferation of local government business regulations after 2001 (discussed below) also impinge on the business environment. These findings are consistent with alternative cross-country survey-based indicators. For example, according to the *2008 Doing Business* Report published by the World Bank, Indonesia ranks 123rd among the 178 economies that were assessed in 2007. The country fares poorly in comparison with regional peers, including Korea, Malaysia and Thailand, and in policy areas related to the ease of starting and closing a business, employing workers and enforcing contracts.

The decentralisation process that started in 2001 is perceived to have had an adverse impact on the investment climate by increasing the burden of business regulations issued by local governments.[4] The devolution of some regulatory and revenue-raising functions to the districts (*kota/kapubaten*) has allowed them to issue business regulations, including licensing requirements, which often conflict with those set by higher levels of government. In addition, local governments have introduced a variety of non-tax levies on businesses. It is estimated that the number of such tax-related regulations rose to some 6 000 between 2000 and mid-2005 (World Bank, 2006a). Whereas many of these regulations deal with changes in local tax rates or in the bases of existing taxes, others do in fact create new ones, some of which impose barriers to inter-regional trade through levies on the movement of goods.[5] This is despite the fact that the central government has the prerogative to restrict the number of sectors liable for local taxation and to issue guidelines for the creation of local taxes and user charges (Law No. 34 of 2000).[6] Also, according to Law No. 32 of 2004, which replaced the original decentralisation Law No. 22 of 1999, local government regulations cannot conflict with those issued by the central government.

Local governments often disguise new taxes in the form of user charges or other non-tax instruments to avoid scrutiny by the central government. It is estimated that only about 40% of the local levies created in 2000-01 were submitted for evaluation and approval by the central government, as required by law, and that only about one-half of these submissions have been effectively reviewed (World Bank, 2006a). Moreover, the proliferation of local levies creates regulatory uncertainty, because about 30% of the newly created instruments submitted for approval by the central government have been annulled. It has been argued that the delegation to the provinces of the authority to issue licenses for limited-liability companies has resulted in longer and costlier delays to start a business (LPEM-FEUI, 2007a). A survey conducted among notaries has shown that almost 45% of respondents find that this delegation of licensing powers has increased the cost of starting a business. This is consistent with the reported increase in the number of days required to start a business from 97 to 105 between 2006 and 2007 according to the World Bank's 2008 *Doing Business* Report.

To the extent that it has increased the number of officials with discretionary power over economic activity, and because it has made regulations more complex, decentralisation is likely to have increased opportunities for corruption.[7] Surveys conducted at the firm level show that bribes and informal payments increase the effective tax burden on the business sector by about 50% and that these payments rise in proportion to the number of business licenses required by local governments. Corruption also creates barriers to domestic trade, because illegal road charges increase transport costs. The most common bribes are for speeding up the issuance of business permits and licenses, for securing contracts and concessions, and for obtaining and renewing the necessary work/immigration permits for expatriates. Incidentally, a survey conducted among manufacturing firms showed that, by mid-2007, almost 90% of responding firms had occasionally or frequently paid a bribe to government officials (LPEM-FEUI, 2007a). Overall, decentralisation is supposed to have increased business uncertainty, which makes the investment climate less predictable.

Indonesia fares rather poorly in international surveys of good governance. The country lagged behind regional peers, such as the Philippines, Thailand and Malaysia, and particularly Singapore, according to the Transparency International indicators of perceived corruption in 2007. This is in spite of progress over the recent past, since investment-climate surveys carried out in Indonesia show a decline in the share of firms stating that national and local corruption poses an obstacle to entrepreneurship (Figure 2.1). Nevertheless, it appears that the impact on business perceptions of efforts to fight corruption may be tapering off: the percentage of survey respondents who think that corruption will decrease in the near future has declined. The surveys conducted by Transparency International show that, in 2005, almost 80% of respondents thought that corruption was going to decrease in the following three years, but that share fell to 22%

in 2007. Of course, the evidence provided in opinion surveys needs to be interpreted with caution: it is difficult to measure corruption accurately, given that most evidence available to date refers to perception indicators, which may not always reflect progress in efforts to improve governance.

Recent policy initiatives to improve the business environment

The authorities are aware of the need to take decisive action in several policy areas to improve the business environment in support of faster growth. An important recent initiative was a strengthening of the country's FDI regime with the enactment of a new Investment Law in 2007 (Box 2.1). The new legislation simplifies regulations, protects property rights and provides tax incentives for investment (Narjoko and Jotzo, 2007). In particular, it ensures, among other things, equal treatment for domestic and foreign investors. Also, equity restrictions on foreign ownership and several sectoral barriers to foreign participation have been relaxed, at least in part, in telecommunications; air transportation and port management; power generation, transmission and distribution; shipping; water supply; and nuclear power generation. Restrictions remain in a few sectors that are considered sensitive to national interests, such as religion, culture, the environment, and small and medium-sized enterprises (SMEs). Moreover, the issuance of a "negative list" to unify existing sectoral restrictions on foreign involvement has rendered regulations more transparent to foreign investors. By and large, there is a general perception among investors that the new law improves considerably upon the previous legislation. Nevertheless, implementing regulations for several provisions of the law are yet to be issued.

Efforts have been made to promote investment opportunities. The authorities have the intention of converting the Investment Co-ordinating Board, created in 1973 essentially as a screening and authorising agency for foreign investment, into a fully-fledged investment promotion agency.[8] They also aim to strengthen the Board to improve co-ordination among the various government agencies involved in investment regulations. They are working towards reducing the number of procedures needed for approval of new investments and intend to cut back the approval period to one month from the current 105 days.

Initiatives are under way at the local government level to facilitate the issuance of business licenses. Several local governments are setting up business licensing centres as a means of dealing with the uncertainty associated with the proliferation of local business regulations. As in other decentralised countries, the licensing process involves many procedures at different government levels. Verification of compliance with zoning rules and health and safety standards, as well as the issuance of tax registration documentation and product- or activity-specific licenses, require involvement not only of the national and local governments, but also of local business associations. One-stop shops (OSSs) have been set up to consolidate the processing of business licenses issued by separate bodies. The Minister of Home Affairs has recently issued general guidelines on how to establish these regional OSSs.[9]

The government intends to provide tax incentives for investment, as stated in the Investment Law. The broad contours of these incentives have already been defined, although the amounts involved and the actual modalities have yet to be set. They would target investors in priority areas, such as remote regions and special economic zones, priority business activities (e.g. infrastructure and R&D), and labour-intensive sectors

---

Box 2.1. **The 2007 Investment Law**

Law No. 25 of 2007 and related regulations unify Indonesia's legal framework for foreign investment. The law improves upon the 1967 foreign investment law and the 1968 domestic investment law. Its main provisions are the following:

Domestic and foreign investors. The Law ensures equal legal status and treatment of domestic and foreign investors. Until then, separate pieces of legislation had regulated national and foreign investment. The Law also scrapped the divestiture provisions that existed for foreign investors in previous legislation (the 1967 Foreign Investment Law).

Investor protection. The Law protects investors against expropriation by stating that owners should be compensated at the market value of assets, should they be seized or nationalised. It also guarantees foreigners the right to make international currency transfers to repatriate earnings, dividends and profits; to purchase inputs or productive capital; to reimburse loans; and to contract for foreign technical assistance.

Dispute resolution. Disputes between the government and foreign investors may be settled by international arbitration.

Negative list. Foreign investment is allowed in all sectors/activities, except for those explicitly listed by the Law. Protected sectors/activities may be "closed" or "open with restrictions". They are closed when they are considered strategic or reserved for small and medium-sized enterprises (SMEs), and open with restrictions when joint-venture provisions, location conditions, ownership caps and special licensing requirements apply.

Land property rights. The Law strengthens property rights by extending the period during which land can be leased. The maximum holding of land for cultivation, building rights and land use is extended from 35, 30, and 25 to 95, 80, and 75 years, respectively.

Immigration procedures. The Law allows greater mobility of foreign professionals. Expatriates may be granted two-year residency permits and multiple-entry visas. After two years of continuous residency, the work permit may be converted into a permanent residency permit.

Tax incentives. The Law provides tax breaks for projects that create employment, promote infrastructure and technological development, and develop rural areas and pioneer industries. Special tax incentives include tax holidays for infant industries and/or innovative enterprises, income tax reductions, exemption or reduction of import duties and value added tax on purchases of capital goods and raw materials, accelerated depreciation for investment, and property tax relief.

Commitment to a reduction of red tape. The Law stipulates the establishment of one-stop-shop (OSS) services for investment applications, and centralises the registration process at the national level, a task assigned to the Investment Co-ordinating Board (BKPM).

---

involving partnerships with SMEs. The main incentive instruments would include income-tax breaks, reductions in import duties on inputs and raw materials, and the introduction of value-added tax holidays for imported capital machinery and equipment not produced locally, as well as reductions in land and building-related taxes.

Anti-corruption efforts are being stepped up. An anti-corruption law was enacted in 1999, following the financial crisis and the change in government (Box 2.2). The government launched a high-profile anti-corruption campaign in 2004 in recognition of the need to take steadfast action to improve governance. More recently, efforts to curb

> ## Box 2.2. **An overview of anti-corruption initiatives**
>
> Anti-corruption legislation was passed in 1999, including the creation of a Commission for Eradication of Corruption (KPTPK). The law was amended in 2001 to deal with issues not covered in the original legislation, including rules on gratuities received by public employees.
>
> Additional measures were taken in 2004. The institutional framework for fighting corruption was strengthened, including through greater autonomy granted to newly created institutions, such as the KPTPK and the Anti-Corruption Court. Existing institutions, such as the Supreme Audit Commission, the Financial Transactions and Analysis Centre (PPTAK) and the Attorney General's Office, were encouraged to become more active in combating corruption. To prevent illicit personal enrichment, high-ranking officials are now required to fill in a personal wealth report, which is an important step in the area of corruption prevention.
>
> Recent initiatives to fight corruption include an increase in budgetary appropriations from 2008 to finance an increase in civil servants' compensation by 20%, the introduction of payment of a 13th monthly salary to civil servants and an increase in the value of food allowances received by civil servants. Budget allocations have also been raised significantly for almost all institutions involved in strengthening governance and law enforcement (Supreme Audit Agency, Supreme Court, Ministry of Law and Human Rights and the Attorney General's Office).

corruption in the public sector have focused on increasing civil servants' compensation and budgetary appropriations for several agencies involved in internal and external control. All in all, anti-corruption efforts seem to be paying off, at least as gauged by a reduction over time in the share of survey respondents stating that national and local corruption is a problem for business development (Figure 2.2). Moreover, the number of corruption investigations and prosecutions increased significantly between 2004 and 2005, including at all levels of governments and State-owned enterprises (World Bank, 2006a).

Indonesia's FDI regime: International comparisons

Despite the recent efforts to liberalise Indonesia's FDI regime, remaining restrictions are relatively burdensome by international comparisons. On the basis of the OECD methodology for assessing the stringency of regulations on FDI, described in Box 2.3, Indonesia's overall score is stricter than those of most countries in the OECD area, except Australia, Iceland and Mexico (Figure 2.3). This implies that those latter three countries impose more restrictions on foreign investment than Indonesia. Nevertheless, Indonesia fares better than the BRICS group of countries, except Brazil and South Africa, suggesting that it is relatively well placed in relation to other major emerging-market economies, which are among the most attractive destinations for FDI outside the OECD area.

On the basis of the OECD indicator, Indonesia's FDI regime is particularly stringent on foreign ownership. Caps on equity holdings are especially restrictive in the transport sector, including air, maritime and surface transport, and in telecoms, mainly with respect to the provision of fixed-line services. With respect to operational and screening requirements, they are less restrictive than in most OECD countries, although bureaucratic hurdles remain on international labour mobility. Although there is no formal restriction on the nationality of Board members, managers and workers in general, the 2007 Investment

> **Box 2.3. The OECD methodology for calculating FDI regulatory restrictiveness**
>
> The restrictiveness of a country's FDI regulations has been calculated for OECD and selected non-OECD countries using a methodology presented in OECD (2006). The scoring methodology intends to measure deviations from national treatment against foreign investment. For example, regulations of labour and product markets that apply equally to both foreign and domestic investors are not considered when calculating the restrictiveness indicators. Only statutory barriers are accounted for; tacit institutional, informal or behavioural restrictions to FDI are therefore excluded.
>
> Restrictiveness is measured on a 0-1 scale, with 0 representing full openness and 1 an outright prohibition of FDI. Three main restrictions are considered: i) limitations on foreign equity holdings; ii) screening and notification requirements; and iii) other restrictions, such as those on management, operations and movement of expatriate workers. Equity restrictions receive the highest weight in the indicator. If foreign equity if banned, the other criteria become irrelevant, and the score reaches its maximum value.
>
> FDI restrictions can apply across the board or only to specific sectors. For each country, the index covers 9 sectors and 11 sub-sectors (in parentheses): i) professional services (legal, accounting, engineering and architectural), ii) telecommunications (fixed and mobile), iii) transport (air, maritime and road), iv) finance (banking and insurance), v) retailing, vi) construction, vii) hotels and restaurants, viii) electricity and ix) manufacturing. Because investment in energy, including oil and gas, varies substantially across countries depending on their natural endowments, energy other than electricity is not covered by the methodology. Restrictiveness is scored at the sectoral level, and a national average is computed using trade and FDI weights.

Figure 2.3. FDI legislation: Cross-country comparisons[1]

Low scores indicate less restriction

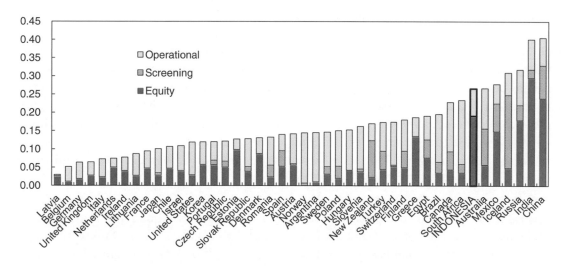

StatLink ⫘ http://dx.doi.org/10.1787/414842843363

1. Refers to the state of legislation in 2007 for Indonesia and in 2006 for all other countries.

Source: OECD (2006) and OECD calculations.

Law states that priority should be given to Indonesian citizens. Also, although foreign workers are allowed to obtain an initial two-year work permit, this is subject to approval by the General Directorate for Migration, based on a request by the Investment Co-ordinating Board.

Dealing with infrastructure bottlenecks

Trends in spending and performance

The development of basic infrastructure was among the authorities' priorities in the 1970s and 1980s. Projects were financed and carried out by the government in areas related to transport, electricity and telecommunications. Total investment in infrastructure building accounted for around 10% of GDP at the time. By 2007 this ratio had fallen substantially, despite a strong recovery since 2000. Government spending on infrastructure development has now recovered, although it still remains below to its pre-crisis level. But private investment has yet to bounce back, a trend that can be explained at least in part by concern over the legal and regulatory environment.

Indonesia has some of the poorest infrastructure development indicators in Southeast Asia (Table 2.1). According to the 2002-03 Global Competitiveness Report, the overall quality of Indonesia's infrastructure was ranked 64th out of the 80 countries surveyed. Moreover, based on national opinion surveys, bottlenecks in energy and transport are the most pressing infrastructure-related obstacles to business development (Figure 2.1). A survey carried out by the World Bank on eleven countries in Asia and Australia placed Indonesia in seventh position regarding clean water supply (World Bank, 2004).

In electricity, access is low even by regional standards, in spite of substantial improvements over recent decades. Efficiency is also poor, as gauged by energy losses in distribution. The likelihood of energy shortages has increased substantially in recent years, given that demand growth has outpaced the expansion of supply. Power outages are particularly detrimental to enterprises in electricity-intensive sectors, such as electronics, chemicals and textiles, because firms must pay for their own generators to secure a steady flow of electricity. Connection to the electricity grid also poses an economic burden on firms, because they have to pay upfront for the installation of meters and related equipment.[10] Production costs have also risen substantially over the recent past, because around 30% of electricity generation is oil-based. Notwithstanding these problems, opinion surveys suggest that business perceptions of the quality and quantity of infrastructure have improved in gas, electricity, water/sanitation and physical road conditions between 2006 and 2007 (LPEM-FEUI, 2007a).

Transportation infrastructure is also poor. Urban roads are severely congested, and several important toll-road projects, such as Jakarta's outer ring-road and the trans-Java highway, have yet to come to fruition. It is estimated that 43% of the road network in Java is congested, a figure that is expected to rise to 55% by 2010, if demand growth continues to outpace that of supply (World Bank, 2007). The quality of national and provincial roads is nevertheless considered to be in line with regional comparators. But district roads tend to lack essential maintenance, and some of the poorest areas of the country, especially the Eastern islands, still lack all-season roads. The costs of owning a motor vehicle are found to be higher in Indonesia than in other Asian countries, due in part to damaged roads (LPEM-FEUI, 2007b). Given Indonesia's geography, port infrastructure is essential for the

Table 2.1. **Selected infrastructure indicators, 1990, 2000 and 2005**

	Indonesia			Southeast Asia	OECD
	1990	2000	2005		
Water/Santitation					
Improved sanitation facilities (per cent of population with access)	46	52	55[1]	50.6[1]	100[1]
Improved water source (per cent of population with access)	72	76	77[1]	78.5[1]	99.5[1]
Energy and transport					
Electric power consumption (kWh per capita)	161.4	400.4	478.2[1]	1 343.5[1]	9 693.5[1]
Electric power transmission and distribution losses (per cent of output)	13.7	10.9	13.4[1]	7.0[1]	6.2[1]
Electricity production composition by source (in per cent)					
Coal	31.5	36.7	40.1[1]	69.1[1]	37.9[1]
Natural gas	2.3	28.2	16.1[1]	2.3	28.2
Oil	42.7	19.1	30.2[1]	41.1	4.3[1]
Other	23.5	16.1	13.6[1]	56.7	71.8
Roads, paved (per cent of total roads)	45.1	57.1	..	..	100[1]
Information and communication technologies					
Fixed line and mobile phone subscribers (per 1 000 people)	6.1	50.1	270.6	496.5	1 324.5[1]
International Internet bandwidth (bits per person)	..	1.2	6.9[1]	97.1	4 731.5[1]
Internet users (per 1 000 people)	0.0	9.2	72.5	88.7	525.4
Personal computers (per 1 000 people)	1.1	10.2	13.9[1]	38.2[1]	585.2[1]

1. Refers to 2004.
Source: World Bank (*World Development Indicators*).

economic integration of distant regions and for facilitating international trade.[11] Overall, poor infrastructure reduces the competitiveness of the manufacturing sector, because it raises operating costs and increases travel time between plants and consumer markets. Logistical costs, including transportation and related charges, may reach as much as 14% of total production costs in Indonesia, against about 5% in the case of Japan (LPEM-FEUI, 2005).

Improvements in water/sanitation infrastructure can yield dividends in terms of poverty alleviation, because poor people tend to have less access to services (Table 2.2). Poor health and the prevalence of water-borne diseases affect the earnings capabilities of vulnerable individuals, who need to take time off work due to illness. At around 30% on average, access to piped water in urban areas is among the lowest in the region, well behind countries such as Malaysia, Philippines, Thailand and Vietnam. Access to waste-water treatment is even lower: it is estimated that only about 1.3% of the population of Jakarta is connected to a sewerage system. The remainder of the population relies on septic tanks, from which untreated sewage often leaks into the ground, polluting water sources and facilitating the spread of communicable diseases. Access to water supply also imposes a financial burden on enterprises, because the PDAMs, the State-owned water companies, use a cost-sharing scheme according to which firms need to bear upfront the full cost of connectivity. As in the case of transport, there are important differences in the quality of infrastructure across the country, with the Eastern provinces typically lagging behind Java-Bali and Sumatra.

To some extent, capacity constraints at the local government level have taken a toll on infrastructure development. Because of skills shortages and limited operational capabilities, local governments have often been unable to take on the spending assignments devolved to them by the central government in the course of decentralisation.

Table 2.2. **Indonesia: Access to infrastructure by income level, 2005**

In per cent of households

	Lowest quintile	Quintile 2	Quintile 3	Quintile 4	Highest quintile
Sources of drinking water					
Piped water	9.3	12.5	16.9	23.8	37.4
Pump	6.5	7.7	9.2	10.7	12.8
Well	50.8	50.1	47.8	43.2	31.1
Spring	22.6	16.8	12.8	9.0	4.4
Other	10.7	12.9	13.3	13.3	14.4
Waste water disposal[1]					
Septic tank	10.0	15.4	23.7	36.6	62.0
Untreated disposal in water bodies (rivers, lakes and ocean)	25.1	25.3	23.8	21.0	12.9
Hole	31.1	30.8	28.0	23.2	14.9
Other	33.7	28.6	24.5	19.2	10.2
Toilet facilities					
Private	40.4	48.6	56.0	67.4	82.5
Shared	14.7	13.7	13.4	12.1	9.0
Other	44.9	37.8	30.6	20.6	8.5
Sources of light[1]					
Electricity supplied by PLN	39.8	50.1	60.1	72.1	87.6
Torch	45.9	36.1	26.4	15.9	4.9
Other	14.3	13.8	13.5	12.0	7.6
Access to ICT					
Fixed line	1.1	2.5	4.5	11.4	38.1
Mobile phone	1.0	3.9	9.0	21.3	55.5
Internet connection	0.1	0.2	0.5	1.3	8.9

1. Refers to 1996.
Source: Susenas and OECD calculations.

This is despite the fact that most investment spending continues to be financed by the centre through intergovernmental transfers according to Indonesia's revenue-sharing system (discussed in Chapter 1). Capacity shortages are thought to be most severe in areas related to project design and development, resulting in implementation delays. A lack of clarity about the spending functions of each government level is another culprit. Moreover, as in other decentralised countries, local governments sometimes do not have incentives to invest in infrastructure, especially when projects create externalities for neighbouring jurisdictions. Finally, the government's anti-corruption efforts, while laudable, are believed to have slowed infrastructure building. This may be an ineluctable short-term cost associated with efforts to enhanced accountability at the local level of government over time. Anecdotal evidence suggests that local officials often fear being charged with misconduct when committing budgetary resources to large investment projects.

Investment in the mining and forestry sectors is also surprisingly low. This is in spite of high commodity prices in recent years and ample potential for development, given Indonesia's abundant natural resources. Before 1998, Indonesia attracted over 5% of the world's mining exploration investment, as opposed to just 0.5% over the recent past. This fall in attractiveness can be attributed to the business climate more generally, including weaknesses in the regulatory framework. High taxes and governance problems, including deficiencies in the enforcement of contracts, have also discouraged investment.

Empirical evidence and recent policy initiatives

There is considerable potential for boosting potential growth by removing existing infrastructure bottlenecks. As discussed in Chapter 1, the link between infrastructure and growth tends to be stronger in lower-income countries, such as Indonesia, where infrastructure deficiencies are most pressing than in more developed countries in the OECD area. But the actual magnitude of the effect of infrastructure development on growth can only be gauged empirically. To shed some light on this issue, the empirical evidence reported in Annex 2.A1 suggests that a 1% improvement in a composite infrastructure indicator is associated with an increase in GDP of nearly 0.9% in the long run. The analysis is based on physical measures of infrastructure in energy, transport and information and communication technology (ICT), instead of estimates of capital stock computed from investment flows. This approach avoids the need to quantify the capital stock, which is not without pitfalls, especially in an environment of volatile inflation, and the difficulties of assessing the efficiency with which private and public inputs are combined to produce infrastructure outputs. Estimation of a strong association between infrastructure development and growth is consistent with previous analysis for Indonesia. For example, simulations conducted by LPEM-FEUI show that increasing electricity generation capacity alone by 5% would boost economic growth by about 0.3 percentage points.

Efforts are under way to encourage private-sector involvement in infrastructure development (Box 2.4). A number of high-profile infrastructure summits have taken place since 2005 to bring together domestic and foreign investors, as well as government officials. These summits have sought to disseminate information on investment opportunities in areas such as transport, electricity, telecommunications, oil and gas, and water/sanitation. The authorities' strategy is to focus on non-economically viable projects, while encouraging the private sector to explore commercially viable investment opportunities. Efforts to improve the regulatory framework in network industries have yielded mixed results. The government enacted a new electricity law in 2002 introducing open competition for power generation from 2007 and abolishing the State-owned company's (PLN) monopoly in distribution by allowing entry of both foreign and domestic private companies. Unfortunately, the law was overturned by the Constitutional Court in 2004. The government is currently drafting a new electricity law but has not yet submitted it to Parliament.

Enterprise access to credit

A shallow financial market makes it difficult for firms, especially SMEs and those operating in the informal sector, to obtain credit at competitive rates. The stock of outstanding credit has risen over the years on the back of an increase in consumption loans until 2006 (Figure 2.4), although credit for investment and working capital recovered somewhat in 2007. Also, at around 21% of GDP in 2007, the credit ratio is lower than in regional comparator countries, such as Malaysia, Thailand and Korea, where credit accounts for more than 100% of GDP. Non-bank credit to enterprises, especially through fixed-income and equity markets, is also limited in Indonesia.

The Indonesian financial sector is comparatively small in relation to regional peers. Banks account for the lion's share of financial institutions' assets, and State-owned banks make up around 35% of bank assets (Table 2.3). Another consideration is that there are limited sources of long-term finance in the banking sector, since nearly all deposits have

---

Box 2.4. **Efforts to encourage private-sector involvement in infrastructure development**

The government launched an Investment Policy Package in 2006 with the aim of boosting institutional capacity and co-ordination among the line ministries dealing with infrastructure development and regulation, such as the ministries of Finance, Energy and Mineral Resources, and Public Works. The Package deals with changes in laws and regulations, and sets policy objectives for fostering competition, eliminating barriers to private participation in infrastructure and improving the regulatory framework. Government support for infrastructure is also evidenced in the 2008 Budget Law, which raised budgetary appropriations for the ministries in charge of infrastructure, especially the ministries of Public Works, Communications, and Energy and Mineral Resources.

As a way of boosting public-private partnerships, the National Committee on Policy for Accelerating Infrastructure Provision (KKPPI) was established in 2005 as an inter-ministerial body. Within the KKPPI, a Public-Private Participation (PPP) Unit was set up as a centre of technical expertise in project preparation, using as a benchmark international best-practice guidelines. In turn, a Risk Management Unit (RMU) was established at the Ministry of Finance to evaluate the projects prepared by the PPP Unit and to deliberate on the allocation of government financial support for private investors. This is with the aim of ensuring appropriate risk sharing between the public and private sectors and dealing with private-sector concerns about the long-term financial viability of projects.

The authorities also agreed to provide credit support for selected infrastructure projects, including a PLN-owned power plant and the Trans-Java toll-road project. In 2006, the government also approved new implementing regulations related to roads, railways, shipping, aviation and utilities. Furthermore, it has promoted the establishment of self-regulatory bodies for the toll roads, oil and gas, telecommunications and water supply. As for land acquisition, which has been the main impediment for toll-road projects, the government has established a new working team to overcome land acquisition problems, and has allocated 600 billion *rupiah* to the infrastructure fund managed by the Government Investment Unit.

---

short maturities (three months or less). The banking sector is also concentrated, with major banks accounting for almost 70% of bank assets. The non-bank segment, which is dominated by pension funds, is developing fast but still has ample scope for further expansion.

Access to credit is particularly difficult for SMEs, especially those operating in the informal sector. This is the case in most countries, not only in Indonesia. Banks are often unable, and unwilling, to lend to borrowers with limited recoverable collateral. For example, despite considerable improvements in some regions, land-property rights are poorly defined, which constrains the ability of small borrowers to use their own property as collateral when applying for loans. When banks do lend, terms and conditions are typically harsher than in the case of larger enterprises or those formally registered. This problem is aggravated by a weak judicial system because of lengthy and costly loan-recovery procedures. Unequal access and terms of credit impose a constraint on the ability of SMEs to break out of a vicious circle of low growth and informality in which they are often trapped. To some extent, these shortcomings may be compensated, at least in part, by information on firms' credit history, which can be used to gauge creditworthiness. But if such information is not easily available to different financial institutions, enterprises

Figure 2.4. **Trends in credit and financial development, 2000-07**

A. Trends in investment and consumption credit[1]

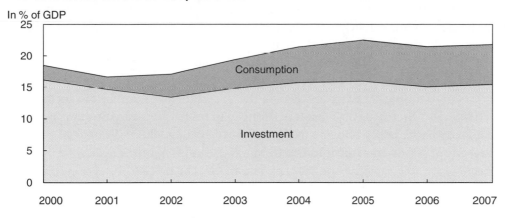

B. Equity and corporate bond markets[2]

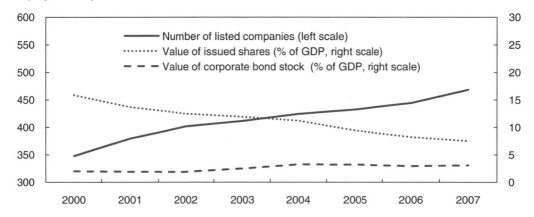

StatLink ⧉ *http://dx.doi.org/10.1787/414876732826*

1. Investment credit includes loans for working capital. Consumption credit includes housing and motor vehicle loans, credit cards and others.
2. The number of listed companies refers to December for all years.

Source: Bank Indonesia.

Table 2.3. **Financial-sector indicators: Cross-country comparisons, 2003**

In per cent of GDP

Sector	Indonesia[1]	Malaysia	Thailand	Singapore
Bank and non-bank assets	**68.1**	293.8	147.6	401.3
Banks	**53.9**	159.8	114.9	233.4
Non-banks	**14.2**	134.0	32.7	167.9
Insurance companies	**2.8**	19.5	3.4	49.8
Pension funds	**4.3**	56.4	4.8	65.7
Mutual funds	**1.1**	20.1	12.2	20.0
Outstanding corporate bonds	**2.3**	38.0[2]	12.3[2]	32.4[2]
Others	**3.7**	0.0	0.0	0.0
Stock market capitalisation	**29.3**	162.2	79.4	162.3

1. Refers to 2005.
2. Refers to 2004.
Source: World Bank (2006b).

become captives of the banks from which they borrow. This reduces the scope for competition among banks, which could facilitate access to, and reduce the cost of, credit.[12]

The strengthening of the banking sector after the 1997-98 crisis has fulfilled an important framework condition for the expansion of credit and the development of the non-bank market segment. As discussed in Chapter 1, conventional indicators, such as the share of non-performing loans in loan portfolios, capital-adequacy ratios and profitability indices, have improved markedly over the years. Whereas before the crisis the banking sector was predominantly privately owned, the government's share in the sector's assets rose considerably thereafter as a result of the need to rescue failing institutions in the wake of the crisis. Recent policy efforts have focused on the upgrading of financial safety nets and the adoption of international banking standards. A limited deposit insurance mechanism has now replaced the blanket guarantee scheme that was put in place at the time of the crisis. A deposit insurance agency has also been created, and Basel II standards will be adopted, starting in 2008 and becoming fully operational by 2010.[13]

The monetary authorities believe that further consolidation in the banking sector would allow banks to reap the benefits of economies of scale. This would result in efficiency gains and lower intermediation costs. Consolidation could also facilitate banking supervision by allowing Bank Indonesia to focus on fewer, larger institutions. To this end, a series of measures have been taken by Bank Indonesia to encourage mergers in the banking system. These include a single-bank-ownership policy (*i.e.* institutional investors can have a majority stake in only one commercial bank), the introduction of tax breaks to encourage bank mergers and a gradual increase in minimum core-capital requirements (from 80 billion *rupiah* in 2007 to 100 billion *rupiah* in 2010).

Measures have also been taken to boost credit. Recent initiatives include a loosening of some prudential regulations: capital requirements have been relaxed through lower risk weights, including for corporate bond holdings, and provisioning and loan classification procedures have been eased for sub-prime borrowers, especially for small enterprises and borrowers that have defaulted on previous credits. Bank Indonesia has introduced a scheme of rising reserve requirements to penalise banks with lower loan-to-deposits ratios. A Banking Policy Package was announced by the central bank in March 2008 to facilitate access to the banking sector by small enterprises. Moreover, State-owned banks have been encouraged to be more active in financing infrastructure projects and in maintaining higher credit growth rates. Finally, registration and licensing procedures have been simplified for banks. The authorities believe that these measures are consistent with concomitant efforts to strengthen banking supervision and reduce systemic risk in the financial sector.

Policy considerations

The overall policy message

The business environment will need to improve in support of private-sector development and growth. There is broad agreement, supported by business surveys, that weaknesses in the regulatory framework, capacity constraints and poor governance are constraining business opportunities and entrepreneurship. A proliferation of onerous regulations by local governments is also weighing on the business environment. This is despite recent efforts, including the latest policy packages for infrastructure and financial-

OECD ECONOMIC SURVEYS: INDONESIA: ECONOMIC ASSESMENT – ISBN 978-92-64-04805-8 – © OECD 2008

sector development, as well as the enactment of the Investment Law in 2007, to strengthen the investment regime.

To be effective, policy action would need to be comprehensive and to create synergies among different policy areas. Consideration could therefore be given to initiatives aimed at strengthening the regulatory framework, including by removing red tape at the local level of government, improving governance and reducing remaining restrictions on foreign investment. This would be consistent with the APEC-OECD Integrated Checklist for Regulatory Reform.[14] Further financial deepening would facilitate access by enterprises to more abundant, cheaper sources of finance.

Improving the business climate

There are options for curtailing the ability of local governments to introduce additional regulations and levies on business activity. Strong political resolve will be needed at the central government level to do so, given that local jurisdictions use this prerogative as a means of raising revenue. At a minimum, the central government could issue a list of business levies that would be deemed acceptable, subject to formal approval. The proposed levies could be collected only once approval has been granted. Any other instrument that might be introduced by the local governments would automatically be considered null and void. For these measures to be effective, it would be important to disseminate information on submissions and approvals broadly and transparently, preferably through the internet site of the Ministry of Home Affairs. At the same time, enforcement would need to be stepped up, because many such levies have been introduced without the accord of the central government.

Much can be done to facilitate compliance with business regulations. To this end, local governments that have not yet done so could be encouraged to set up one-stop shops (OSSs) in their jurisdictions. Currently only 284 of the 440 *kota* and *kapubaten* have such facilities in operation. This is despite the Minister of Home Affairs issuing regulations in July 2006 (Decree No. 24) instructing local governments to set up OSSs within a year. In addition, user satisfaction surveys could be carried out systematically, preferably by the central and local governments in conjunction with local business associations, to make sure that the budgetary resources devoted to these services are well spent and in line with the needs of the business community. This is important, because the range of services provided through OSSs varies significantly across local governments, and best practices can be learned and disseminated more effectively. Moreover, the use of information and communication technologies (ICTs) for the purpose of business registration could be encouraged.[15] These efforts would also potentially reduce the scope of corruption, because face-to-face encounters would be replaced by on-line procedures, making it potentially more difficult for officials to solicit and/or be offered bribes in exchange for services.

The fight against corruption should continue. Recent efforts in this area are laudable. But specific sanctions could be introduced for different offenses. Co-ordination could also be stepped up among different layers of government in the areas of prevention and enforcement. In particular, while preventive efforts have already been made in many areas, they could be strengthened. This is the case, for example, of the requirement that civil servants submit personal wealth reports, because only 54% of senior government officials had done so by 2005, and only a small share of these reports have been audited. These reports could be made available to the public, which would contribute to enhancing transparency and accountability.

The legal system could be strengthened. The protection and enforcement of contracts would be a priority for improvement. Tangible results in this area would be important to attract foreign investment, particularly in sectors or activities that depend on transfers of new technologies and intellectual property in general. Allegations of discrimination against foreign companies in the court system remain a source of concern. More generally, there is a fairly general perception that the legal system is slow and imposes an additional cost on businesses.

Attracting more and better FDI

Consideration could be given to a further relaxation of remaining barriers to foreign investment. In particular, foreign-ownership constraints in selected sectors may have a detrimental impact on the quality of FDI. While intended to encourage technology transfers from multinationals, this requirement may in fact discourage such transfers, because foreign investors may be wary of losing intangible assets to local partners. This may be especially the case in technology-intensive sectors, such as fixed-line telephony, where foreign equity participation is capped at 49%. Empirical evidence suggests that productivity tends to be higher in majority-owned foreign firms, once other standard determinants are taken into account.[16] Also, the findings reported in Annex 2.A2 show that, together with the share of government-owned capital, foreign ownership increases enterprise spending on royalties, R&D and human capital development.

There is some scope for strengthening the Investment Co-ordinating Board. To this end, the possibility of transferring the prerogative of appointing the Head of the Board to Parliament, rather than the executive branch of government (the President), as currently stated in the 2007 Investment Law, could be considered as a way of guaranteeing greater stability in investment policies.

The cost effectiveness of the tax incentives to be put in place in accordance with the new Investment Law will need to be assessed judiciously. The same applies to the tax expenditures associated with the new special economic zones that the government intends to create to boost economic activity, investment and employment in remote areas.[17] There are many reasons to worry about cost effectiveness. On the one hand, tax incentives may be associated with deadweight losses, because they may benefit firms that would invest anyway, regardless of whether those incentives are available or not. On the other, by reducing the after-tax return on investment, such incentives divert savings to finance comparatively less profitable projects. In addition, the merits of sector-specific legislation, as opposed to across-the-board incentives that would not discriminate in favour of specific investments, would need to be taken into account in policy discussions. A final consideration is related to the reduction of import duties, which are currently restricted to capital goods, machinery and equipment that are not produced domestically. The possibility of broadening these incentives to imports that compete with locally produced capital goods and intermediate inputs could be evaluated as a means of fostering competition in these sectors.

Policy efforts to boost human capital accumulation would have the additional payoff of removing an obstacle to foreign investment in knowledge-intensive sectors. Studies show that technology transfers through FDI have been limited in Indonesia due to capacity constraints to absorb foreign technologies, including skills shortages.[18] These weaknesses will need to be tackled, if Indonesia is to diversify its exports from primary and labour-intensive goods towards manufactured goods with higher value added. At the same time, efforts to develop infrastructure, especially in transport and telecommunications, would contribute to bolstering Indonesia's attractiveness to foreign investment in an environment of heightened competition for FDI, especially among regional peers.

Removing infrastructure bottlenecks

Intergovernmental fiscal relations need to be strengthened in support of public investment. An improved fiscal position has created, and will likely continue to create, room in the budget for increasing budgetary appropriations for investment projects in general and for infrastructure development in particular (discussed in Chapter 1). At the same time, the alleviation of skills shortages at the local government level would remove existing constraints on the implementation of investment projects, as noted above. Policy co-ordination could also be enhanced among local governments in areas where inter-jurisdictional spillovers might discourage individual action. Finally, a clarification of spending assignments across government levels would reduce uncertainty, which discourages local governments from investing.

The regulatory framework needs to be strengthened to remove obstacles to private-sector involvement in the electricity sector. As discussed in Chapters 1 and 3, the existence of price subsidies for fuel and electricity, despite cuts over the years, has had a detrimental impact on investment in the energy sector. Private-sector involvement is discouraged by price management, because it is difficult for investors to assess rates of return on projects, and by existing restrictions on equity ownership, discussed above. Decisive action is therefore needed to remove these obstacles if the authorities expect the private sector to be an important partner in infrastructure development. The design of a new regulatory framework would obviously be a complex task. But, at a minimum, it would include the liberalisation of prices and entry into the generation, transmission and distribution segments of the energy market and the introduction of an independent regulator in the sector. An increase in electricity supply would certainly have a significant effect on welfare for the poorer members of society. This is because they lack access to electricity, which makes it about six times more expensive for them to obtain energy compared to those who do have an electricity connection (LPEM-FEUI, 2003).

There are important challenges in the water/sanitation sector, where investment in infrastructure development is extremely low. As in the case of energy, the main obstacle to private-sector involvement is of a regulatory nature. Prices are set at unrealistically low levels, which do not allow for full cost recovery. The consequent financial losses imposed on the utility companies (PDAMs) have therefore curtailed their ability to invest. The option of liberalising prices and entry into the sector, as well as setting up an independent regulator, would be a much-needed first step towards encouraging private-sector investment. Again, the regulatory challenges associated with a comprehensive overhaul of the current system should not be underestimated.

Promoting further financial deepening

Indonesia fares poorly in conventional indicators of financial development, even in comparison with regional peers. This suggests that there is considerable scope for further financial deepening. Credit has expanded briskly in recent years, aided by favourable global financial conditions until recently, the strengthening of the banking sector after the financial crisis and a gradual reduction in real interest rates in an environment of continued disinflation. But more could to be done to encourage further credit growth in a manner that is consistent with financial resilience and the conduct of monetary policy under inflation targeting. Efforts in this area would go in the direction of unlocking additional sources of finance for investment by facilitating access to credit by the underserved population, especially poor individuals and SMEs, which often operate in the informal sector and have limited recoverable capital to be used as collateral for bank loans. Survey-based information shows that insufficient collateral is among the main reasons why firms are unable to borrow from formal financial institutions.

The merits of further consolidation in the banking sector could be re-evaluated. The Indonesian banking system is already fairly concentrated. The authorities are right that a multitude of small banks creates challenges for banking supervision. But the scope for further consolidation to boost efficiency through gains in economies of scale needs to be weighed against the risk that additional concentration might weaken competition among banks, which would most likely result in less favourable lending conditions for individuals and enterprises (OECD, 2001; Amel *et al.*, 2004). The monetary authorities are advised to carefully assess these risks and to factor in the costs to the budget of the tax breaks that have been introduced to encourage mergers and acquisitions in the banking sector.

More could be done to reduce the presence of State-owned banks in the financial system. Of course, the rescue of financial institutions in distress after the 1997-98 crisis explains to a large extent the rise in the share of bank assets accounted for by State-owned banks. More generally, as in many other emerging-market economies in the OECD area and beyond, strong government involvement in the financial sector was originally justified by the need to correct market failures and to channel directed credit to selected economic sectors and activities. But, in a progressively more liberal economic environment, the case for continued government ownership of commercial banks becomes less compelling. The full privatisation of these banks could therefore be considered.

Initiatives to develop the non-bank sector would be welcome. The pension and mutual fund industry, as well as insurance, have benefitted from macroeconomic adjustment since the 1997-98 crisis, supportive global financial conditions and a reduction in interest rates in recent years. But existing regulatory barriers could be removed to foster further development in these market segments. These include regulatory barriers to entry in the insurance sector, which hamper competition. Foreign ownership in the insurance industry is capped at 80% by the 2007 Investment Law. This cap is perceived as overly stringent, because local companies often lack the capital for the remaining 20% needed to set up a joint venture with a foreign partner. Also, capital requirements are higher for entrants than for companies already operating in the market. This increases entry costs and gives a competitive advantage to incumbents. The possibility of increasing the equity ownership cap set by the Investment Law to the 99% level applicable to banks could be considered as a way of fostering the development of the non-bank sector.

A summary of policy considerations is presented in Box 2.5.

Box 2.5. **Summary of policy considerations for improving the business and investment climate**

Options for improving the business climate

- Central government control over the issuance of business regulations by local governments could be tightened.

- Business regulations could be simplified and rendered more user-friendly. Local governments could be encouraged to set up one-stop shops.

- Ongoing anti-corruption efforts could be enhanced through the introduction of specific sanctions for all individual offenses.

Attracting more and better FDI

- Remaining foreign-ownership constraints could be relaxed further in several sectors as a means of boosting private investment.

- The cost effectiveness of the tax instruments allowed for in the Investment Law could be assessed.

- Tax-related incentives for investment could be broadened to include a reduction in import duties for capital goods and intermediate inputs that compete with domestic production.

Removing infrastructure bottlenecks

- Intergovernmental fiscal relations need to be strengthened in support of public investment, including by clarifying spending assignments across levels of government.

- The regulatory framework needs to be enhanced in network industries, especially energy and water/sanitation, to encourage private-sector involvement in infrastructure, including by liberalising prices and entry.

Promoting further financial deepening

- The merits of further consolidation in the banking sector could be re-evaluated against the risk that further consolidation might weaken competition among banks.

- The option of privatising State-owned banks could be considered to reduce the government's presence in the banking sector.

- Foreign-ownership restrictions in the insurance industry could be relaxed in support of the development of the non-bank sector.

Notes

1. See Takii and Ramstetter (2005) for more information.

2. See BKPM (2007) for more information.

3. The Index, based on survey responses from the 1 000 largest companies around the world that were responsible for 70% of FDI in 2005, focuses on the impact of political, economic and regulatory changes affecting FDI intentions. See ATKearney (2005 and 2007) for more information.

4. A survey performed in 2003 showed that around 40% of firms found that regulatory uncertainty increased after decentralisation (Asian Development Bank, 2005).

5. The fact that the salary of members of sub-national legislatures is linked to local tax collection is thought to be one of culprits for the proliferation of local taxes and levies.

6. The law is sometimes unclear. For example, it stipulates that local taxes should not run counter to the public interest and should not have a negative impact on the local economy, which is difficult to ascertain in practice. The objectives set in the law for local tax policy are the following: i) local governments should tax relatively immobile bases; ii) there should be no sharing of tax bases

among the different levels of government; *iii*) local taxes should be elastic with respect to regional income; *iv*) local taxes should follow principles of equity and ability to pay by local residents; and *v*) local taxes should safeguard the environment.

7. The association between fiscal decentralisation and corruption is complex and depends, among other things, on how sub-national spending is financed. See de Mello and Barenstein (2001) for a review of the literature and empirical evidence for a cross-section of countries. Also, Bardhan (1997) shows that under "decentralised corruption", bribery may be more widespread than in "centralised corruption".

8. The Investment Co-ordinating Board is in charge of designing investment policy, including by identifying potential investment opportunities; issuing norms, regulations, standards and procedures; promoting partnerships between the business and academic communities; disseminating information to boost competition; and fostering co-ordination among the different levels of government, regulatory agencies and the central bank.

9. International organisations, such as the Asia Foundation and the German Technical Co-operation (GTZ), have also been working with local jurisdictions to improve the performance of OSSs in areas related to management capacity, licensing practices and the application of information and communication technology to business registration.

10. In particular, firms are required to buy their own transformers in a cost-sharing scheme: they pay lower electricity fees for some agreed period of time, after which ownership of the transformer is transferred to PLN and the firms start paying the normal fee.

11. Poor port infrastructure has contributed quite significantly to an increase in average waiting time for loading and unloading activities in ports (Patunru *et al.*, 2007).

12. Recognising the need to take action in this area, Bank Indonesia launched a Debtor Information System (DSI) in 2005. DSI initially covered borrowers with loans above 50 million *rupiah*, which excluded small enterprises, but was subsequently extended to all loans.

13. The new deposit insurance scheme is funded by a bi-annual payment of 0.1% of bank deposits and government resources. The deposit insurance agency is responsible for the resolution and management of failed banks. A co-ordinating committee including representatives of Bank Indonesia, the Ministry of Finance and the deposit insurance agency decides if a failed bank is of systemic importance or deserves liquidation.

14. See OECD (2005) for more information.

15. The experience of the Sragen district in Central Java is instructive. Sragen is the only local jurisdiction in the country currently offering one-stop services to have an ICT system in operation. The Integrated Service Agency was set up in 2002 to connect 20 district offices to the local government's headquarters. The system is expected to be expanded to 208 sub-districts and villages by the end of 2008.

16. These hypotheses are by and large supported by empirical evidence. Productivity is higher in foreign-owned or controlled firms, once other determinants of productivity are taken into account (Thomsen, 1999; Takii and Ramstetter, 2005). By contrast, smaller multinationals are less prone to transfer technology from parent firms, so that their labour productivity levels are comparable to those of domestic firms. In addition, Blalock and Gertler (2008) find that technology transfers from multinationals to upstream firms lead to less concentration, lower prices and higher output growth in downstream firms. Borensztein *et al.* (1998) find that FDI crowds in domestic investment because of complementarities in production. For Indonesia, Blomström and Sjöholm (1999) find that labour productivity in domestic firms increases with foreign participation in the sector where these firms operate, suggesting the presence of intra-industry spillovers from FDI to domestically owned establishments.

17. The special economic zones envisaged by the government include not only the Batam, Bintan and Karimun islands near Singapore, but also Bali, Makassar and Bitung. The intention is to streamline administrative, tax and customs procedures to encourage investment in these regions.

18. Human capital facilitates technology transfers and enhances the capacity of local workers to assimilate foreign technology and know-how. See Borensztein *et al.* (1998) and Lim (2001) for more information. Agiomirgianakis *et al.* (2006) also find that, apart from human capital, infrastructure constitutes an important FDI attractor in the OECD area. Thomsen (1999) states that technology transfers from FDI have taken place mainly through on-the-job training and have been limited to basic skills in Indonesia.

Bibliography

Agiomirgianakis, G.M., D. Asteriou and K. Papathoma (2006), "The Determinants of Foreign Direct Investment: A Panel Data Study for the OECD Countries", *Working Paper*, No. 3, City University, London.

APEC-OECD (2005), "Integrated Checklist on Regulatory Reform: A Policy Instrument for Regulatory Quality, Competition Policy and Market Openness", APEC-OECD Co-operative Initiative on Regulatory Reform, OECD, Paris.

Asian Development Bank (2003), "Country Governance Assessment Report, Republic of Indonesia", Asian Development Bank, Manila.

Asian Development Bank (2005), "Improving the Investment Climate in Indonesia", Asian Development Bank, Manila.

ATKearney (2005), "FDI Confidence Index 2005", *Global Business Policy Council*, Alexandria, VA.

ATKearney (2007), "FDI Confidence Index 2007", *Global Business Policy Council*, Alexandria, VA.

Bardhan, P. (1997), "Corruption and Development: A Review of Issues", *Journal of Economic Literature*, Vol. 3, pp. 1320-46.

BKPM (2007), "Statistics of Direct Investment. Monthly Report, October", Investment Co-ordinating Board, Jakarta.

Blalock, G. and P.J. Gertler (2008), "Welfare Gains from Foreign Direct Investment through Technology Transfer to Local Suppliers", *Journal of International Economics*, forthcoming.

Blomström, M. and F. Sjöholm (1999), "Technology Transfer and Spillovers: Does Local Participation with Multinationals Matter?", *European Economic Review*, Vol. 43, pp. 915-23.

Borensztein, E., J. de Gregorio and J.-W. Lee (1998), "How Does Foreign Direct Investment Affect Economic Growth?", *Journal of International Economics*, Vol. 35, pp. 115-35.

Calderon, C. and L. Serven (2004), "The Effects of Infrastructure Development on Growth and Income Distribution", *Policy Research Working Paper*, No. 3400, World Bank, Washington, DC.

de Mello. L. and M. Barenstein (2001), "Fiscal Decentralisation and Governance: A Cross-Country Analysis", *Working Paper*, No. 01/71, International Monetary Fund, Washington, D.C.

Lim, E.-G. (2001), "Determinants of, and the Relation Between, Foreign Direct Investment and Growth: A Summary of the Recent Literature", *Working Paper*, No. 175, International Monetary Fund, Washington, D.C.

LPEM-FEUI (2003), "Study on the Impact of Increases in the Fuel Price and Electricity Tariff", Joint Report, Institute for Economic and Social Research, University of Indonesia, and Energy Analysis and Policy Office, USAID, Jakarta.

LPEM-FEUI (2005), "Inefficiency in the Logistics of Export Industries: The Case of Indonesia", Joint report, Institute for Economic and Social Research, University of Indonesia, and Japan Bank for International Cooperation, Jakarta.

LPEM-FEUI (2007a), "Investment Climate Monitoring. Round IV", Institute for Economic and Social Research, University of Indonesia, Jakarta.

LPEM-FEUI (2007b), "Domestic Trade Barrier: The Case of Transportation Costs in Indonesia", Joint report, Institute for Economic and Social Research, University of Indonesia, World Bank and Asia Foundation, Jakarta.

Narjoko, D. and F. Jotso (2007), "Survey of Recent Developments", *Bulletin of Indonesian Economic Studies*, Vol. 43, pp. 143-69.

OECD (2006), "OECD's FDI Regulatory Restrictiveness Index: Revision and Extension to More Economies", *Working Paper on International Investment*, No. 2006/4, OECD, Paris.

Patunru, A.A., N. Nurridzki and Rivayani (2007), "Port Competitiveness: A Case Study of Semarang and Surabaya, Indonesia", in D. Brooks and D. Hummels (eds), *Infrastructure's Role in Lowering Asia's Trade Costs: Building for Trade*, Asian Development Bank, Manila.

Takii, S. and E.D. Ramstetter (2005), "Multinational Presence and Labour Productivity Differentials in Indonesian Manufacturing, 1975-2001", *Bulletin of Indonesian Economic Studies*, Vol. 41, pp. 221-42.

Thomsen, S. (1999), "Southeast Asia: The Role of Foreign Direct Investment Policies in Development", *OECD Directorate for Financial, Fiscal and Enterprise Affaires Working Paper*, No. 1, OECD, Paris.

World Bank (2004), "Averting an Infrastructure Crisis: A Framework for Policy and Action", The World Bank Office, Jakarta.

World Bank (2006a), "Revitalizing the Rural Economy: An Assessment of the Investment Climate Faced by Non-Farm Enterprises at the District Level", World Bank, Washington, D.C.

World Bank (2006b), "Unlocking Indonesia's Domestic Financial Resources", World Bank, Washington, D.C.

World Bank (2007), "Spending for Development: Making the Most of Indonesia's New Opportunities. Indonesia Public Expenditure Review 2007", World Bank, Washington, D.C.

ANNEX 2.A1

Infrastructure investment and economic growth

This Annex uses principal component and co-integration analyses to assess the relationship between investment in infrastructure development and economic activity in Indonesia. If indicators of infrastructure development and GDP are found to co-integrate, at least one of them should adjust over time in response to movements in the other one to maintain a stable relationship between them. Once the existence of a stable relationship is established, the direction of causality is assessed.

Measuring infrastructure development

Information is not readily available on public and private expenditure on infrastructure development or on the value of a country's stock of infrastructure capital. Indonesia is no exception. In addition, emphasis on expenditure flows as a measure of infrastructure development would neglect the efficiency with which investment in infrastructural development are designed and implemented. The empirical analysis reported below therefore focuses on conventional output indicators, such as the coverage of a country's transport and telecommunications networks, as well as its energy generation and distribution capabilities. A focus on these three sectors is due to data availability.

Principal component analysis will be used to reduce the set of potential infrastructure output indicators to a tractable number of common factors.* It is not possible to include all potentially relevant indicators in the estimating equation, because they far outnumber the degrees of freedom needed to obtain the relevant parameter estimates. Also, these indicators are highly collinear, which weakens their individual predictive power.

The indicators used to extract the principal components are available from the World Bank's *World Development Indicators* database. They cover quantity and quality indicators in three sectors: energy (indicators of total electricity production, shares of electricity production from hydropower and from oil, the extent of electric power transmission and distribution losses, electric power consumption, value of energy imports and use, volumes of combustible renewables and waste), transport (number of air transport passengers) and information and communications technology (number of fixed line and mobile phone subscribers, value of telecom investment and revenue, number of employees in the

---

* Principal component analysis is useful in data reduction. It has been used in the empirical analysis of infrastructure and growth by Calderon and Serven (2004), among others. According to the technique, the leading eigenvectors from the eigen decomposition of the covariance matrix of the variables under consideration describe a series of uncorrelated linear combinations of those variables that contain most of the variance in the data.

telecom sector, number of telecom mainlines and subscribers). Only the indicators for which information was available for at least 30 years (to maximise the number of observations) and which were found to be normally distributed were retained. The sample spans the period 1970-2006. The two components whose eigenvalues were found to explain nearly all the variation in the data were retained.

Testing for unit roots and co-integration

Real GDP, per capita GDP and the two factors computed on the basis of the principal component analysis were tested for the presence of unit roots using the ADF test. The results for the GDP series show that the real GDP and per capita GDP series follow I(1) processes in levels (with or without a linear time trend). The results of the test carried out on the two infrastructure factors show that one of them (F1, defined in logarithmic form) follows an I(1) process in levels (with or without a linear time trend), whereas the other (F2) was found to be stationary in levels. F2 was therefore dropped from the analysis, since it cannot co-integrate with the GDP series.

The Johansen-Juselius test was performed on the levels of the GDP and F1 series. In this case, a system $X = (GDP, F1)$ can be written in error-correction form as $A(L)\Delta X_t = \Pi X_{t-1} + u_t$, where, as usual $\Pi = \alpha\beta'$, β' is the vector of co-integrating coefficients, α is the vector of loading coefficients, $A(L)$ is the distributed lag operator, and u_t is a multivariate white-noise process. The results of the co-integration tests, reported in Table 2.A1.1, show that there are at most one co-integrating vector on the basis of the trace and maximum eigenvalue statistics. Infrastructure is positively signed in the co-integrating vector (normalised on GDP), suggesting that a 1% improvement in the composite indicator of infrastructure is associated with an increase in GDP by nearly 0.9%, regardless of whether GDP is defined in per capita terms or not. These high long-term returns would suggest that infrastructure is under-provided.

The results of the weak exogeneity tests are also reported in Table 2.A1.1. The procedure consists of imposing a restriction on the loading parameters, such that the full hypothesis that the i-th row of α is zero can be tested. If the null hypothesis cannot be rejected, then the i-th endogenous variable is found to be weakly exogenous with respect to β. On the basis of this test, GDP was found to be weakly exogenous, but not the indicator of infrastructure development. These findings suggest that causality runs from GDP to infrastructure development in the long term, regardless of whether GDP is defined in per capita terms or not.

Table 2.A1.1. **Infrastructure development and economic activity:
Co-integration tests, 1970-2006**[1]

(Dep. Vars.: Real GDP or Real GDP per capita and infrastructure, in logs)

	Real GDP		Real GDP per capita	
Co-integration tests				
Ho: rank = p	Eigenvalue	Trace	Eigenvalue	Trace
p == 0	26.83**	35.272**	12.449**	14.852**
p <= 1	8.44	8.44	2.40	2.40
Number of lags	2		2	
Deterministic component	Intercept		No	
Co-integration vector				
Normalised vector (on real GDP)	(1, -0.88)		(1, -0.90)	
Weak exogeneity tests:[2]				
Real GDP is exogenous: Ho: (0,a)	0.33		0.05	
	[0.57]		[0.81]	
Infrastructure is exogenous: Ho: (a,0)	14.88		9.59	
	[0.00]		[0.00]	

1. Refers to the Johansen-Juselius cointegration tests. (**) indicates statistical significance at the 5% level. The sample spans the period 1970-2006.
2. Based on the estimated co-integrating vector of rank equal to one and distributed as chi-squared, with one degree of freedom (p-values in brackets).

Source: World Bank (*World Development Indicators*) and OECD estimations.

ANNEX 2.A2

Enterprise expenditure on royalties, R&D and labour training: Firm-level evidence

This Annex reports empirical evidence based on firm-level data on how capital structure affects enterprise expenditure on royalties, R&D and labour training. Data are available from the *Statistik Industri* Survey carried out by BPS on an annual basis. The Survey covers a large number of manufacturing establishments and provides detailed information on output, investment, capital, assets and expenditure, with a breakdown by production and nonproduction workers. The 1997 wave is used, because it features a special module on workers' educational attainment and enterprise expenditure on innovation.

The regressions

The determinants of firms' expenditure on royalties, R&D and labour training (in 100 000 *rupiah*) are estimated using the Tobit regression model. This is the appropriate econometric technique to use, because the dependent variable is censored, and linear estimation methods would lead to biased estimations. The independent variables are the share of capital owned by the government and by foreign investors (the omitted reference category is the share of capital owned by domestic firms), measures of enterprise size (value of capital and number of employees), the educational level of workers (proxied by the percentage of workers with at least tertiary education), location (province where the enterprise is located) and type of product. Errors are clustered at the provincial level to allow for the possibility that firms located in the same province have correlated disturbances.

The results

The results, reported in Table 2.A2.1, show that enterprise expenditure on royalties, R&D and labour training rises with the share of capital owned by the government and by foreign investors. Foreign ownership has a stronger impact on expenditure on royalties than government ownership. But the converse is true for expenditure on R&D and labour training.

Regarding the control variables, enterprise size (measured by both capital and number of employees) is positively associated with all three spending categories. The quality of human capital at the firm level is also positively associated with spending on royalties, R&D and labour training. This may be due to the fact that a more skilled labour force increases the rates of return on innovation and labour training. Finally, the significance of some of the product and provincial dummies confirms the existence of inter-sectoral and geographical disparities in the determinants on innovation and labour training.

Table 2.A2.1. **The determinants of expenditure on royalties, R&D and labour training, 1997[1]**

	Expenditure on:[2]		
	Royalties	R&D	Labour training
Share of government-owned capital	0.068**	0.061***	0.031***
	(0.027)	(0.018)	(0.006)
Share of foreign capital	0.237***	0.040***	0.019***
	(0.039)	(0.006)	(0.002)
Total capital[2]	0.004***	0.002**	0.001**
	(0.001)	(0.001)	(0.000)
Number of workers	0.003**	0.002***	0.001***
	(0.001)	(0.001)	(0.000)
Share of workers with at least tertiary education	0.432***	0.260***	0.101***
	(0.086)	(0.073)	(0.020)
Product dummies			
Textiles	−2.245	−2.275***	−0.282
	(2.027)	(0.561)	(0.177)
Wood products	0.781	−1.002*	0.313**
	(0.888)	(0.578)	(0.137)
Paper and pulp	4.496*	−1.623***	0.288**
	(2.610)	(0.613)	(0.122)
Chemicals, rubber, plastics, coke, refined petroleum	6.167***	1.651**	0.512***
	(1.666)	(0.640)	(0.170)
Other non-metallic mineral products	−3.624**	−1.230	−0.215
	(1.782)	(0.903)	(0.168)
Basic metals and metal products (except machinery and equipment)	−4.568	4.065	1.180*
	(3.372)	(2.878)	(0.637)
Machinery and equipment	7.376***	0.249	0.571***
	(2.705)	(0.361)	(0.208)
Furniture	1.525	−0.759	0.333
	(1.492)	(0.745)	(0.355)

1. All regressions are estimated by Tobit and include provincial dummies (not reported). Statistical significance at the 1, 5 and 10% levels is denoted by (***), (**) and (*), respectively. Robust standard errors clustered at the provincial level are reported in parentheses.
2. Defined in 100 000 *rupiah*.
Source: Statistik Industri data and OECD estimations.

ISBN 978-92-64-04805-8
OECD Economic Surveys: Indonesia: Economic Assesment
© OECD 2008

Chapter 3

Improving labour market outcomes

Since the financial crisis of 1997-98 job creation has slowed, unemployment has been high, particularly among youths, and informality remains widespread. Important contributory factors are a tightening of employment protection legislation (EPL), especially with the enactment of the Manpower Law of 2003, and sharp increases in the real value of the minimum wage. Strict EPL is nevertheless failing to provide effective social protection for the needy, because it is not binding in the informal sector. It is also affecting Indonesia's trade competitiveness, because the country has a comparative advantage in labour-intensive manufacturing, whose former dynamism has waned.

This chapter argues that options for reform could focus on making labour legislation more flexible, particularly for regular contracts, while enhancing formal safety nets, especially through well targeted, conditional income-transfer programmes.

Indonesia has suffered from slow job creation, pervasive informality and persistently high unemployment since the 1997-98 crisis. The rebound in economic growth, especially since 2004 (discussed in Chapter 1), has therefore failed to deliver a commensurate improvement in labour-market performance. To a large extent, this outcome is associated with a tightening of employment protection legislation (EPL), following the enactment of a new labour code in 2003 and a substantial increase in the real value of the minimum wage since 2001. Indonesia's labour code is characterised by burdensome dismissal procedures and onerous severance compensation entitlements, even in relation to countries in the OECD area.

While a tightening of EPL over the years was aimed essentially at protecting workers from adverse economic shocks, it has failed to boost social protection and to promote economic efficiency. This is because a more restrictive labour code has protected relatively better-off workers in the formal sector to the detriment of those with a more tenuous attachment to the labour market, such as women, youths and the less educated. A more restrictive labour code is also likely to have hurt Indonesia's trade competitiveness, given the country's comparative advantage in labour-intensive manufacturing, a sector that has lost dynamism. Enterprises operating in the formal sector are likely to have substituted skilled labour and capital for unskilled labour in response to rising costs associated with progressively more onerous labour legislation.

This chapter reviews trends in employment, labour-force participation, unemployment and informality, as well as in poverty and income distribution. Emphasis is placed on the main provisions of Indonesia's labour code, including minimum-wage entitlements, that are likely to have held back improvements in labour-market outcomes. The chapter's key policy message is that a combination of greater flexibility in EPL and more effective social-insurance and assistance programmes would better equip Indonesia to meet the demands for enhanced social protection while making greater use of available labour inputs in support of faster sustainable growth.

Labour-market trends

Trends in labour-force participation, employment, unemployment and informality

On the basis of Indonesia's National Labour Market Survey (*Sakernas*), labour-force participation has been fairly stable over time at about two-thirds of individuals aged at least 15 years (Table 3.1). In comparison with OECD countries, labour supply is fairly low among women, although it is slightly higher for men (Figure 3.1). Participation is somewhat lower than in the OECD area for prime-age individuals (aged 25-54), reflecting a comparatively low rate for women, but is much higher for older workers (aged 55-64). This latter finding most probably reflects the precariousness of formal social insurance in Indonesia (Box 3.1), which limits the ability of older workers, especially those who have worked predominantly in the informal sector, to save for retirement. With regard to female participation, there are cultural reasons why women may prefer not to work outside the home, but international experience suggests that a lack of affordable child care makes it

Table 3.1. **Trends in labour-force participation, unemployment and employment, 1996 and 2004**

In per cent, individuals aged 15 years and above

	1996				2004			
	Labour force participation	Employment	Unemployment	Informal sector[1] (in % of employment)	Labour force participation	Employment	Unemployment[2]	Informal sector[1] (in % of employment)
Total	**66.1**	**62.6**	**5.3**	**65.4**	**65.0**	**60.7**	**6.7**	**69.6**
By gender								
Males	82.7	78.9	4.6	61.1	83.5	78.6	5.8	67.7
Females	49.9	46.7	6.5	72.5	46.7	42.9	8.2	72.9
By age								
15-24	50.9	42.6	16.4	57.7	50.0	39.0	22.1	58.8
25-54	76.5	74.7	2.4	64.1	74.2	71.8	3.2	68.5
55-64	66.1	65.9	0.3	83.3	63.5	63.1	0.6	88.4
65+	40.3	40.2	0.2	89.8	39.7	39.6	0.2	95.5
By residence								
Rural	71.7	69.4	3.2	77.2	69.8	67.1	3.9	86.3
Urban	58.8	53.8	8.6	45.7	60.1	54.2	9.9	48.7
By education								
No schooling	67.6	67.0	0.9	82.4	63.5	62.8	1.2	92.2
Primary	67.5	65.7	2.7	74.2	66.6	64.9	2.6	84.4
Lower secondary	51.4	47.9	6.9	62.6	55.9	51.7	7.5	72.2
Upper secondary	71.2	61.4	13.8	34.2	68.9	58.7	14.8	41.0
Tertiary	86.3	76.3	11.6	12.4	85.3	77.3	9.4	15.9

1. The informal-sector is defined as including all self-employed and unpaid workers.
2. Calculated using the same definition as in 1996. The unemployment rate reported by BPS for 2004 is much higher, at 9.9%, because it includes discouraged workers. The labour force participation rate consistent with this alternative definition of unemployment is 68.6%.
Source: Sakernas and OECD calculations.

difficult for women with young children to reconcile household and professional activities. Moreover, the participation rate is higher in rural than in urban areas, reflecting the tendency for all household members to work in family plots. Finally, labour supply also tends to rise with educational attainment, as it does in OECD countries.

Employment patterns are comparable to those of labour supply. It tends to be higher for males than females, for residents of rural areas than urban dwellers, and among prime-age individuals than youths and elderly workers. Employment also rises with educational attainment. Moreover, there was a slight fall in employment rates during 1996-2004, except for the most educated individuals. In any case, labour mobility does not appear to be constrained by the proliferation of regulatory barriers among the local jurisdictions since decentralisation in 2001 (discussed in Chapters 1 and 2).

Unemployment is particularly high for youths, workers with secondary education and women. It increased substantially during 1996-2004, albeit from a small base, for older workers and for the least educated individuals (i.e. those with no schooling). By contrast, although it remains high, unemployment fell significantly among individuals with tertiary education, reflecting a rising demand for skilled labour to the detriment of less educated workers. To a certain extent, high unemployment among the workers who would otherwise be best equipped to find a job in the formal sector suggests that these individuals may be reticent to work in the informal sector. When faced with a job loss, they

Figure 3.1. **Labour force participation by age and gender: Cross-country comparisons, 2004**

Countries ranked by participation rate for prime-age females

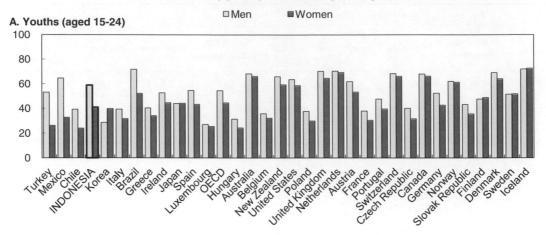

A. Youths (aged 15-24)

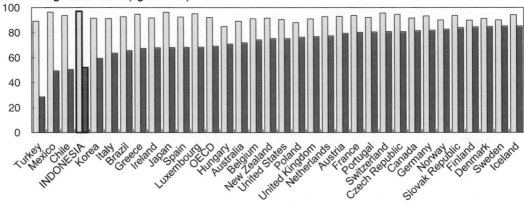

B. Prime-age individuals (aged 25-54)

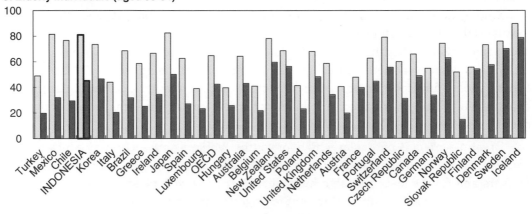

C. Elderly individuals (aged 55-64)

StatLink http://dx.doi.org/10.1787/415018736002

Source: *Sakernas*, INE for Chile, IBGE for Brazil, OECD (*Labour Force Statistics*) and OECD calculations.

Box 3.1. **Social security in Indonesia**

The current system

Formal social-security arrangements are in their infancy in Indonesia. A programme launched in 1992 (*Jamsostek*) offers old-age pensions, life and health insurance, and job-related disability and illness compensation to private-sector workers (and their families) employed in firms with more than 10 employees or payroll of more than one million *rupiah*. Participation in health insurance is optional, if the enterprise has alternative arrangements. Separate mandatory regimes are in place for civil servants (*Taspen*) and for the police and armed forces (*Asabri*).

The largest mandatory programme, *Jamsostek*, is financed predominantly through employers' contributions. Coverage for disability, life and health insurance is financed entirely by employers' contributions (7.24-11.74% of gross monthly earnings, depending on job-related disability coverage), while old-age pensions are financed jointly by employers and employees. Employees contribute 2% of gross monthly earnings. Contributions are paid into a fund managed entirely by a State-owned company, while health care can be provided by private institutions, so long as they are able to at least match the coverage of services provided publicly.

The main shortcomings of *Jamsostek* are that it covers only formal-sector workers and that compliance is very low. Because the vast majority of Indonesian workers have informal-sector jobs and/or are employed in small firms, they are not covered by the scheme. According to the Ministry of Manpower and Transmigration, only about one-fifth of the employed population was enrolled with *Jamsostek* in 2002. Also, the ILO estimates that only about one-half of employers required to enrol in the scheme are actually enrolled.

The value of old-age pensions financed through *Jamsostek* is also low. Leechor (1996) estimates that the average replacement rate is only about 7-11% of a worker's final basic salary after 35 years of active work (against 100% for *Taspen* retirees). More recent estimates show that the gross replacement rate for male average earners with 35 years' contributions was 15.4% in 2006 (OECD, 2008a). Another study conducted by ILO found that the annual average value of a *Jamsostek* pension is only about 5.5 months of average basic salary or 8.5 times the minimum monthly wage (International Labour Organisation, 2003).

The 2004 Social Security Law (*Jamsosnas*)

A National Social Security Law was enacted in 2004, but its relevant provisions have not yet been regulated.* The law extends contributory social security-arrangements to informal-sector workers and the self-employed. The scheme would be publicly-run and cover old-age and survivors' pensions, as well as death and disability insurance. Contributions would be subsidised for poor individuals, defined as those whose income is below the minimum wage. A minimum pension would be set at 70% of the statutory minimum wage. The retirement age would be only 55 years, and workers would be eligible for a pension after as little as 15 years of contribution. Contribution rates are not yet known.

Although the main provisions of *Jamsosnas* have yet to be regulated, several of its provisions appear to be overly generous. The retirement age and the length of contribution required for eligibility for an old-age pension would put considerable strain on the budget, as well as the cost of the contribution subsidy for poor individuals. It is also uncertain whether or not the benefit of social security coverage would create strong enough incentives for informal-sector workers and the self-employed to participate in the scheme.

* See Arifianto (2004) for more information.

may prefer to wait for a formal job, instead of working informally, so long as they can support themselves and their families in the meantime.

Labour informality is widespread. Of course, there is no universally accepted definition of informality (Box 3.2). But for the purpose of the empirical analysis to be reported below, only individuals aged 15-65 years and working as dependent employees will be treated as formal. The self-employed and unpaid workers will therefore be considered informal. Other definitions of informality also include salaried workers in

---

Box 3.2. **Defining labour informality in Indonesia**

There is no universally accepted definition and measurement of labour informality, even in the OECD area. In some countries, the concept of informality is closely related to social security coverage.* In others, informality is defined on the basis of the worker's labour market status and occupation. Definitions are therefore typically country-specific and are not without shortcomings.

A definition based on social-security coverage is often used in countries that already have relatively well developed social insurance mechanisms. This approach is nevertheless problematic for the purpose of cross-country comparisons, because there is considerable variation across countries in the generosity of social-protection entitlements. These include severance payment obligations, unionisation rights, workplace safety regulations, and health and unemployment insurance, among others. In some cases, for example, access to social security is universal. In others, including Indonesia, entitlements are closely linked to labour-market status.

According to the definition of informality based on labour-market and occupational status, workers are considered informal if they are employed in low-productivity, precarious jobs. Employees of small-scale, often family-based enterprises, as well as the self-employed, are therefore typically considered informal. The problem with this definition is that it would treat own-account white-collar professionals as informal, while these individuals are likely to be well educated and to work in high-productivity occupations. For example, the International Labour Organisation (2003) treats as informal the employees of small, private, non-agricultural, unregistered, unincorporated enterprises with less than five paid workers producing at least part of their output for sale or barter.

In the case of Indonesia, a social-security-based definition of informality would make little sense, because the country has only very limited formal retirement schemes and no unemployment insurance. A definition based on labour-market status would therefore be more appropriate. For the purpose of the empirical analysis reported in this chapter, all self-employed (own-account, with or without assistance) individuals aged 15-65 are considered informal. This definition is somewhat more general than that used by Suryahadi *et al.* (2003), who treat as informal all self-employed workers, except for those who are assisted by permanent or non-permanent employees (except in agriculture). A slightly more restrictive definition is that of BPS, according to which the self-employed without assistance and working in professional, leadership and managerial jobs are treated as formal-sector workers.

Despite these differences in definition, informality is widespread. According to the definition used in this chapter, informality accounted for about 65% of employment in 1996, against about 62% on the basis of the definition used by Suryahadi *et al.* (2003).

* See OECD (2004a and 2007a), Maloney (2004) and Gasparini and Tornarolli (2007) for more information.

---

agriculture, a sector that accounts for the bulk of employment (Table 3.2). In any case, based on the definition used in this chapter, nearly 70% of the employed population would be considered informal in 2004. Informality is less widespread among men than women, workers living in rural than urban areas, and among prime-age individuals. As expected, informality declines with educational attainment.

Table 3.2. **Composition of employment by occupation, 1996 and 2004**

In per cent

	1996	2004
Professionals	4.0	4.3
Management	0.3	0.4
Public administration	6.2	5.9
Sales and trade	18.6	18.5
Services	4.7	6.6
Agriculture	41.9	41.4
Production	24.1	23.0
Other	0.4	0.0

Source: Sakernas and OECD calculations.

Empirical evidence on the determinants of employment and earnings

Empirical evidence confirms that employment is strongly affected by educational attainment. The empirical evidence reported in Annex 3.A1 is based on data available from Sakernas for 1996 and 2004. The analysis takes labour informality into account by considering that workers may face three labour-market outcomes: unemployment or no participation, employment in the informal sector and employment in the formal sector. The empirical analysis shows that a worker's probability of working in the formal sector rises with educational attainment, an effect that became stronger in 2004 relative to 1996. Age and marital status are additional powerful predictors of an individual's employment status. Older workers and married individuals are more likely to be employed in the formal sector and less likely to be unemployed or outside the labour force than their younger, single counterparts. Living in rural areas strongly reduces the probability of working in the formal sector and of being unemployed or outside the labour force. Regional effects are also important, although they changed somewhat during the period because of shifting patterns of economic activity within the country.

As in the case of employment, human capital is a strong determinant of earnings too. The analysis reported in Annex 2.A1 sheds additional light on the determinants of earnings by taking into account the "selection bias" that arises from the possibility that individuals may opt for working in the informal sector. The results of the estimations show that formal-sector earnings are strongly affected by the worker's educational attainment. Gross returns to education, measured by the marginal increment in earnings associated with additional academic qualifications, also appear to have risen over time, at least for individuals with tertiary education on the basis of comparisons of the regression results for 1996 and 2004. The results from the earnings equation are as follows: wages rise with age (albeit in a non-linear manner); women are paid less than men, although this effect seems to have waned during 1996-2004; being married is associated with a wage premium in the labour market; workers are better paid in industry than in agriculture or services;

there are important regional effects on earnings; and living in rural areas is detrimental to a worker's earnings prospects.

Overall, the empirical findings suggest that individuals perceive informality as an alternative to unemployment or to staying out of the labour force. Those workers with the best qualifications in terms of schooling and experience (measured on the basis of age) are most likely to find a job in the formal sector. They are also least likely to be unemployed or outside the labour force and most willing to accept a job in the informal sector instead of being unemployed. Their earnings capabilities are also highest. Duality in the labour market is likely to affect labour utilisation adversely by constraining the ability of less-educated workers to break away from a vicious circle of low productivity, low social protection and low earnings. To the extent that a large share of the working-age population is trapped in this vicious circle, the scope for raising and sustaining long-term economic growth through productivity gains is severely constrained.

Duality in the labour market is also detrimental to equity and the business climate. There are several reasons why this is so. *First*, informality creates challenges for the design of social protection programmes, because it makes it difficult to reach informal workers through social assistance and active labour market policies. This is an important consideration in a country such as Indonesia, which is beginning to strengthen its formal safety nets and social protection programmes, and where unemployment has been stubbornly high. *Second*, labour-market duality complicates the design of tax policy, because it narrows tax bases, resulting in a shift of the tax burden onto formal enterprises and individuals. This tax-shifting effect is at odds with efforts to improve the business climate, discussed in Chapters 1 and 2. *Finally*, because informal-sector workers also tend to work in unregistered enterprises, the link that often exists between business and labour informality is strengthened further. Typically, informal enterprises do not have access to the financial system on comparable terms to their formal-sector counterparts, which results in a low level of physical capital used in production and correspondingly low productivity and wages.

Employment protection legislation

The 2003 Manpower Law

Enactment of the Manpower Law of 2003 was a landmark in Indonesia's labour relations.[1] The Law deals with a broad range of issues, including employment protection legislation (EPL), labour training and social security. It also consolidates previous legislation, making the labour code more transparent and systematic. The provisions of the Manpower Law that are most likely to affect the restrictiveness of EPL are related to dismissal procedures, severance pay, temporary work arrangements and minimum wage entitlements. In particular:

● Employers are required to seek authorisation for dismissals from the local Manpower Department (Institution for Settlement of Industrial Relations Disputes). In the case of dismissals due to violations of work rules, bargaining agreements or the terms of individual contracts, employers must issue three warnings within six months of each other before applying for a dismissal authorisation. There are no additional requirements for collective dismissals.

● Severance and long-term service payments are due to workers as compensation for layoffs associated with economic reasons, enterprise bankruptcy, voluntary dismissals following an enterprise takeover, minor offenses, retirement, death, and disability or chronic illness. No severance and long-service pay is due in the case of dismissals due to major offenses (*i.e.* theft, violent behaviour, drunkenness, etc.). The standard severance pay is calculated as one month of salary per year of service (capped at 9 months). In the case of dismissals for economic reasons, retirement, death or disability, severance pay entitlement is doubled. Long-term service pay is calculated as one month of salary for every three years of service, starting with two months' pay for the first three years of service. Total compensation is capped at 10 months' pay after 24 years of service, because compensation for over 21 years of service is also calculated as two months' pay every three years of service.[2]

● Flexible work arrangements (temporary work, fixed-term contracts and sub-contracting) are limited. Temporary work is allowed for three months, which is the statutory duration of probation in long-term contracts. Fixed-term contracts are limited to three years, comprising an initial two-year contract plus a single one-year extension. Sub-contracting is also limited to three years and for workers performing non-core activities. It is also allowed for workers performing one-off tasks or engaged in seasonal work or in jobs related to the introduction of new projects/products.

Minimum wage entitlements

The minimum wage is applicable for regular, full-time work. It is set on an annual basis at the province level on the basis of an estimated cost of living indicator (KHL), which is used as an initial benchmark. This indicator was introduced in the late 1990s and is defined in terms of caloric intake. Since decentralisation in 2001, the level of the minimum wage has been calculated at the local government level (*kapubaten/kota*) and then proposed to the provincial government by a tri-partite wage council, including representatives from labour, government and the private sector. Typically, the lowest minimum wage proposed by the local governments in a province's jurisdiction is chosen by the provincial government.[3]

Minimum wage provisions have been tightened over time. Prior to decentralisation, the minimum wage used to be set nationally by the central government on the basis of an estimated needs indicator (KHM), which corresponds to a lower caloric intake benchmark than that implied by KHL (2 600 as opposed to 3 000 calories per day in the case of KHL). The value of the minimum wage has also risen substantially in real terms on average over the years, especially during 2000-03, having now exceeded its pre-crisis levels (Figure 3.2). The minimum wage also rose faster in real terms than value added per employee, especially during the 1990s and 2000-03. As a result of this increase, the minimum wage is now very high in relation to the median wage in comparison with the countries in the OECD area.

The devolution of minimum-wage setting to the local governments has had a bearing on the relative value of the minimum wage across the country. Until 2000 there appears to have been a process of gradual reduction in disparities in the value of the minimum wage, with higher real increases in the local governments and provinces where the minimum wage had the lowest values in 1988. However, decentralisation seems to have put a halt to this process of convergence (Figure 3.3). The rate of change in the value of the minimum wage in real terms no longer correlates strongly with the level of the minimum wage in the post-2001 period.

Figure 3.2. **Minimum wage trends**

A. Trends in minimum wage and labour productivity, 1987-2006

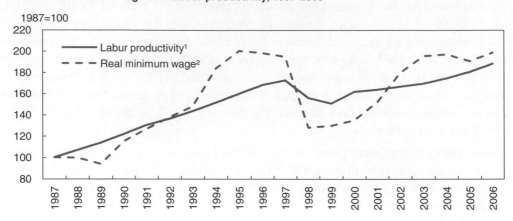

B. Ratio of minimum wage to median wage, 2004[3]

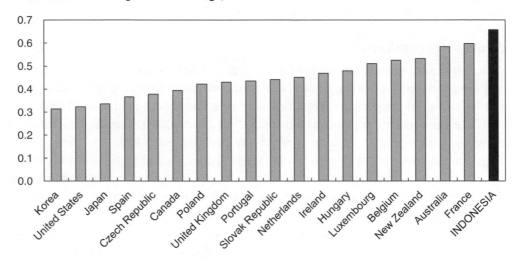

StatLink ⟨⟨⟩⟩ http://dx.doi.org/10.1787/415050300573

1. Defined as gross value added divided by total employment deflated by the GDP deflator.
2. Defined as the simple average of the province/district-level minimum wages deflated by the GDP deflator.
3. For Indonesia, the median wage is calculated for all individuals aged 15-65 working at least 40 hours per week.

Source: Ministry of Manpower, World Bank (*World Development Indicators*) and OECD calculations.

Assessing the restrictiveness of Indonesia's labour legislation

Calculating the OECD EPL indicator

The OECD methodology for constructing an index of EPL strictness focuses on regular employment, collective dismissals and regulations of temporary work (Box 3.3). The estimates for Indonesia are based on responses by the Indonesian government to a standard questionnaire and additional information available from other sources (summarised above). In addition to the OECD countries reported in Table 3.3, the methodology has been applied to date to four countries outside the OECD area (Chile, Brazil, India and South Africa).

On the basis of the OECD methodology, the Indonesian labour code is characterised by restrictive provisions on regular contracts – arising predominantly from bureaucratic

OECD ECONOMIC SURVEYS: INDONESIA: ECONOMIC ASSESMENT – ISBN 978-92-64-04805-8 – © OECD 2008

Figure 3.3. **Minimum-wage setting and decentralisation, 1988-2006**

A. Before decentralisation[1]

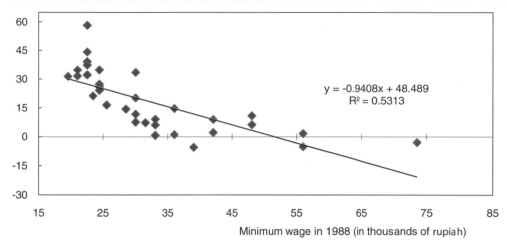

Real change in minimum wage during 1988-2000 (%)

$y = -0.9408x + 48.489$
$R^2 = 0.5313$

Minimum wage in 1988 (in thousands of rupiah)

B. After decentralisation[1]

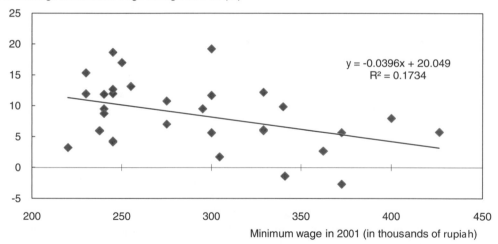

Real change in minimum wage during 2001-06 (%)

$y = -0.0396x + 20.049$
$R^2 = 0.1734$

Minimum wage in 2001 (in thousands of rupiah)

StatLink http://dx.doi.org/10.1787/415077522274

1. The diamonds refer to the minimum wage at the provincial level. Average yearly changes are deflated by the GDP deflator.
Source: Ministry of Manpower; World Bank (*World Development Indicators*); *Sakernas* and OECD calculations.

dismissal procedures and costly severance-pay requirements – and a lack of flexibility in the use of temporary and fixed-term contractual arrangements (Table 3.3). In particular, the need for authorisation from a third party and lengthy notification procedures create considerable procedural delays for the termination of regular contracts. On the other hand, unlike a number of OECD countries, the Indonesian labour code does not impose additional constraints on the termination of employment contracts in the event of collective dismissals.

Box 3.3. **The OECD methodology for assessing EPL restrictiveness**

The OECD methodology for constructing an index of strictness of employment protection legislation (EPL) focuses on regular employment, collective dismissals and regulations of temporary work. The EPL index ranges between 0 and 6, with 0 indicating the lowest and 6 the highest level of rigidity. The methodology used to calculate the EPL index is based on OECD (1999 and 2004a).

The OECD EPL index aims at quantifying the burden of regulatory provisions on employers in a cross-country comparable manner. It is mostly based on labour legislation but also tries to take into account judicial practices and court interpretations of legislative and contractual rules. Employment protection is assessed according to 18 elementary items covering three areas: i) employment protection of individual workers against individual dismissal; ii) specific requirements for collective dismissals; and iii) regulations of temporary employment (fixed-term contracts and temporary work agencies). The main component of the EPL index is on the protection of employees with permanent contracts against individual dismissal, because it is the most common employment arrangement in OECD countries.

On the basis of information on a country's labour legislation, which is collected by sending a standard questionnaire to the country authorities and complemented from additional sources, a four-step procedure is used to compile cardinal summary indicators of EPL strictness. The 18 elementary items, expressed in different units (i.e. time or a score on an ordinal scale), are converted into cardinal scores ranging from 0 to 6. Subsequently the detailed scores are weighted to calculate three sets of summary indicators as more aggregated measures of EPL rigidity. In the final step, an overall summary indicator is calculated based on the three underlying groups: regulations of permanent contracts, rules on temporary contracts and collective dismissals. The latter is attributed a lower weight than the former two (2/12 compared to 5/12, respectively), as collective dismissals reflect only additional employment protection linked to the collective nature of the dismissal.

The EPL scoring methodology does not cover a number of aspects of employment protection that are difficult to quantify. This is the case of the length of trial or probationary periods, which is often not provided in individual contracts or collective agreements. Probationary and notice periods, as well as severance compensation, can be extended by contractual arrangements in many cases. The experience of OECD countries suggests that contractual provisions are likely to play a key role in countries with low levels of statutory employment protection, in particular with regard to severance pay provisions. Judicial practices also affect the outcome of labour disputes, which can deviate from legal provisions, therefore affecting the stringency of labour legislation. The role of trade unions and collective agreements in shaping labour relations is also difficult to gauge. Finally, aspects related to non-wage costs and minimum wage legislation are not taken into account in the EPL index.

The Indonesian legislation is also comparatively stringent with regard to temporary and fixed-term contracts. This is because of ceilings on the duration and number of extensions of such contracts, in addition to restrictions on the nature of the activities and occupations for which such flexible arrangements can be used. Minimum wage provisions are not covered by the OECD methodology for assessing the restrictiveness of a country's EPL, but Indonesia's are shown below to be costly.

Table 3.3. **Employment protection legislation: Cross-country comparisons**[1]

Scores (0-6), countries are ranked from lowest to highest overall rigidity

	Termination of indefinite contracts				Collective dismissals (additional procedures)	Temporary jobs[4]	Overall score[5]
	Procedural inconveniences[2]	Notice and severance pay	Difficulty of achieving dismissal[3]	Average			
United States	0.0	0.0	0.5	0.2	2.9	0.3	0.7
South Africa	0.8	1.3	2.0	1.4	0.2	0.6	1.0
United Kingdom	1.0	1.1	1.3	1.1	2.9	0.4	1.1
Canada	1.0	1.0	2.0	1.3	2.9	0.3	1.1
New Zealand	2.0	0.4	2.7	1.7	0.4	1.3	1.3
Ireland	2.0	0.8	2.0	1.6	2.8	0.6	1.4
Australia	1.5	1.0	2.0	1.5	2.9	0.9	1.5
Switzerland	0.5	1.5	1.5	1.2	3.9	1.1	1.6
Slovak Republic	2.0	2.7	2.8	2.5	2.5	0.4	1.6
Hungary	1.5	1.8	2.5	1.9	2.9	1.1	1.7
Japan	2.0	1.8	3.5	2.4	1.5	1.3	1.8
Chile	1.0	2.8	3.3	2.3	0.0	2.0	1.8
Denmark	1.0	1.9	1.5	1.5	3.9	1.4	1.8
Korea	3.3	0.9	3.0	2.4	1.9	1.7	2.0
Netherlands	3.0	1.9	3.0	2.6	3.0	1.2	2.1
Czech Republic	3.5	2.9	2.8	3.1	2.1	1.1	2.1
Finland	2.8	1.0	2.8	2.2	2.6	1.9	2.1
Austria	2.5	0.9	3.8	2.4	3.3	1.5	2.2
Brazil	0.0	2.2	2.0	1.4	0.0	3.9	2.2
Poland	3.0	1.4	2.3	2.2	4.1	1.8	2.3
Italy	1.5	0.6	3.3	1.8	4.9	2.1	2.4
Spain	2.0	3.5	3.3	2.9	3.1	1.8	2.5
Germany	3.5	1.3	3.3	2.7	3.8	1.8	2.5
Belgium	1.0	2.4	1.8	1.7	4.1	2.6	2.5
Norway	2.0	1.0	3.8	2.3	2.9	2.9	2.6
Sweden	3.0	1.6	4.0	2.9	4.5	1.6	2.6
Indonesia	**6.0**	**2.5**	**1.5**	**3.3**	**0.0**	**3.4**	**2.8**
France	2.5	1.9	3.0	2.5	2.1	3.6	2.9
Greece	2.0	2.2	3.0	2.4	3.3	3.3	2.9
India	4.5	2.5	2.3	3.1	5.8	2.0	3.1
Mexico	1.0	2.1	3.7	2.3	3.8	4.0	3.2
Portugal	3.5	5.0	4.0	4.2	2.9	2.8	3.4
Turkey	2.0	3.4	2.3	2.6	2.4	4.9	3.5
Luxembourg	2.5	2.0	3.3	2.6	5.0	4.8	3.9
Memorandum items:							
OECD average	2.0	1.7	2.7	2.1	3.0	1.8	2.1
OECD emerging-market average[6]	2.3	2.2	2.7	2.4	2.8	2.1	2.4

1. Refers to the state of legislation in 2006 for all countries, 2003 for Chile, 2004 for Brazil and 2007 for India, Indonesia and South Africa.
2. Refers to procedures and delays before giving notice.
3. Refers to valid reasons, possible probationary period before new workers are entitled to protection, compensation for unjustified dismissal, extent of reinstatement.
4. Refers to fixed-term contracts and temporary-work agencies. For Chile and Mexico, the scores estimated for fixed-term contracts are taken to apply to temporary-work agencies as well.
5. The following weights are used: indefinite contracts: 5/12; collective dismissals: 2/12; and temporary jobs: 5/12.
6. Includes Czech Republic, Hungary, Korea, Mexico, Poland, Slovak Republic and Turkey.
Source: OECD (2003, 2004a, 2004b, 2007b and 2008b) and OECD calculations.

Table 3.4. **EPL stringency, 2008**

2008 *Doing Business* indicators, country ranks in ascending order of stringency

	Difficulty of hiring index	Rigidity of hours index	Difficulty of firing index	Rigidity of employment index	Non-wage labour cost (% of salary)	Firing costs (weeks of wages)
Indonesia	**72.0**	**0.0**	**60.0**	**44.0**	**10.0**	**108.0**
OECD	25.2	39.2	27.9	30.8	20.7	25.7
Regional benchmarks						
East Asia and Pacific	19.2	20.8	19.2	19.7	9.4	37.8
South Asia	23.6	17.5	40.0	27.0	6.7	66.0
ASEAN[1]	24.0	22.2	27.8	24.8	8.7	53.4
India	0.0	20.0	70.0	30.0	17.0	56.0
China	11.0	20.0	40.0	24.0	44.0	91.0

1. Includes Brunei Darussalam, Cambodia, Indonesia, Laos, Malaysia, Philippines, Singapore, Thailand and Vietnam.
Source: World Bank (*Doing Business*, 2008).

Comparison with alternative indicators of EPL stringency

The Indonesian labour code is also considered to be stringent in comparison with regional peers and OECD countries on the basis of the World Bank's *Doing Business* indicators (Table 3.4). These comparisons highlight the cost of severance compensation (for a worker having 20 years of service), which is much higher in Indonesia than in any country grouping, although it is also relatively high in China and India. Non-wage labour costs are nevertheless low in relation to OECD countries, but not against regional comparators, with the exception of China and India. The cross-country comparisons also point to a difficulty of hiring workers in Indonesia in relation to OECD countries and regional peers.

Indonesia's labour code is more restrictive than those of regional peers in terms of the duration of the working week and statutory overtime compensation. For example, the country's statutory 40-hour working week is shorter than in most comparator countries in Southeast Asia, where 44-48 hours tend to be standard (Asian Development Bank, 2005). Overtime pay, currently at 150% of the regular hourly remuneration for the first overtime hour and 300% thereafter, is also onerous by comparison with regional peers.

EPL over time

EPL is an important instrument to protect workers in the event of dismissal in countries that do not have comprehensive unemployment insurance. But, the main consideration in Indonesia is that provisions have been tightened over time. Also, the increase in the minimum wage over the years (discussed below) has also raised the cost of severance pay financed by the employer, because severance and long-term service pay is often based on the minimum wage. The labour code was due to be reviewed in 2005-06, but no progress has been made on this matter.

Notwithstanding this increased stringency, compliance with the labour code is likely to have increased over time. Evidence in this area is essentially anecdotal, given that, by definition, it is very difficult to ascertain the level of compliance. But greater protection of trade union rights since the 2000 law that regulates trade union activities,[4] the 2004 law on industrial relations[5] and enhanced efforts on the part of the labour authorities to enforce the legislation are believed to have contributed (Manning and Roesad, 2007).

The impact of minimum wage legislation on earnings and employment

Earnings

In theory, the minimum wage truncates the earnings distribution. It brings those workers whose wages were previously below the minimum statutory level up to it and possibly creates spillover effects for workers who earn more, but not much more than, the minimum wage. In practice, these effects can be gauged by comparing the earnings density functions for employees in 1996 and 2004 using *Sakernas* data.[6] Both distributions are similar, but the peak around the ratio of actual earnings to the minimum wage appears to have shifted slightly to the right (Figure 3.4). At the same time, the share of workers earning less than the minimum wage seems to have fallen. These findings are consistent with the hypotheses of increased compliance over the years and of the existence of spillover effects on those workers whose incomes are just above the minimum wage. Evidence of a positive impact of the minimum wage on earnings is also reported by Rama (2001) and Suryahadi *et al.* (2003).

The extent to which minimum wage legislation affects earnings varies according to gender and age. Male employees earn more than females and are less affected by the minimum wage. This is because the mode of the earnings distribution, depicted in Figure 3.4, is above the minimum wage for males and below it for females. Likewise, prime-age and older individuals (aged 25-65) are better paid and less affected by the minimum wage than youths (aged 15-24). In addition, there are more females than males and more youths than older workers earning less than the statutory minimum. This finding does not imply *per se* that women are discriminated against in the labour market. But the evidence reported in Annex 3.A1 on the basis of household survey data does suggest that women appear to have a negative wage premium, even after controlling for other observable individual and labour-market characteristics that influence earnings.

With regards to educational attainment, the minimum wage appears to have a stronger impact on the earnings distribution for less educated individuals. Again, the spike in the earnings distribution coincides with the minimum wage in the case of less educated employees (*i.e.* those having completed up to lower-secondary education), which suggests a stronger impact of the minimum on earnings than in the case of better educated individuals. Because human capital is strongly correlated with occupation, those individuals working in relatively labour-intensive sectors, such as construction, are more likely to be affected by the minimum wage than their counterparts in sectors whose production requires higher skilled labour.

Employment

The literature suggests that individuals with weak attachment to the labour market are most likely to be affected adversely by minimum wage legislation. Females, less educated individuals, those working in labour-intensive sectors and youths are often more at risk of job losses or of being trapped in the informal sector in the event of sharp increases in the minimum wage. In theory, the minimum wage would lead to job losses if it were set above a market-clearing level. Displaced workers would remain unemployed, if they had other means of supporting themselves, such as access to unemployment insurance; otherwise, they would work informally.

There is nevertheless considerable controversy over the expected impact of minimum wage legislation on employment on both theoretical and empirical grounds. To a certain

Figure 3.4. **The minimum wage and earnings distribution, 1996 and 2004**

Density functions, in multiples of the minimum wage for all employees working at least 30 hours per week

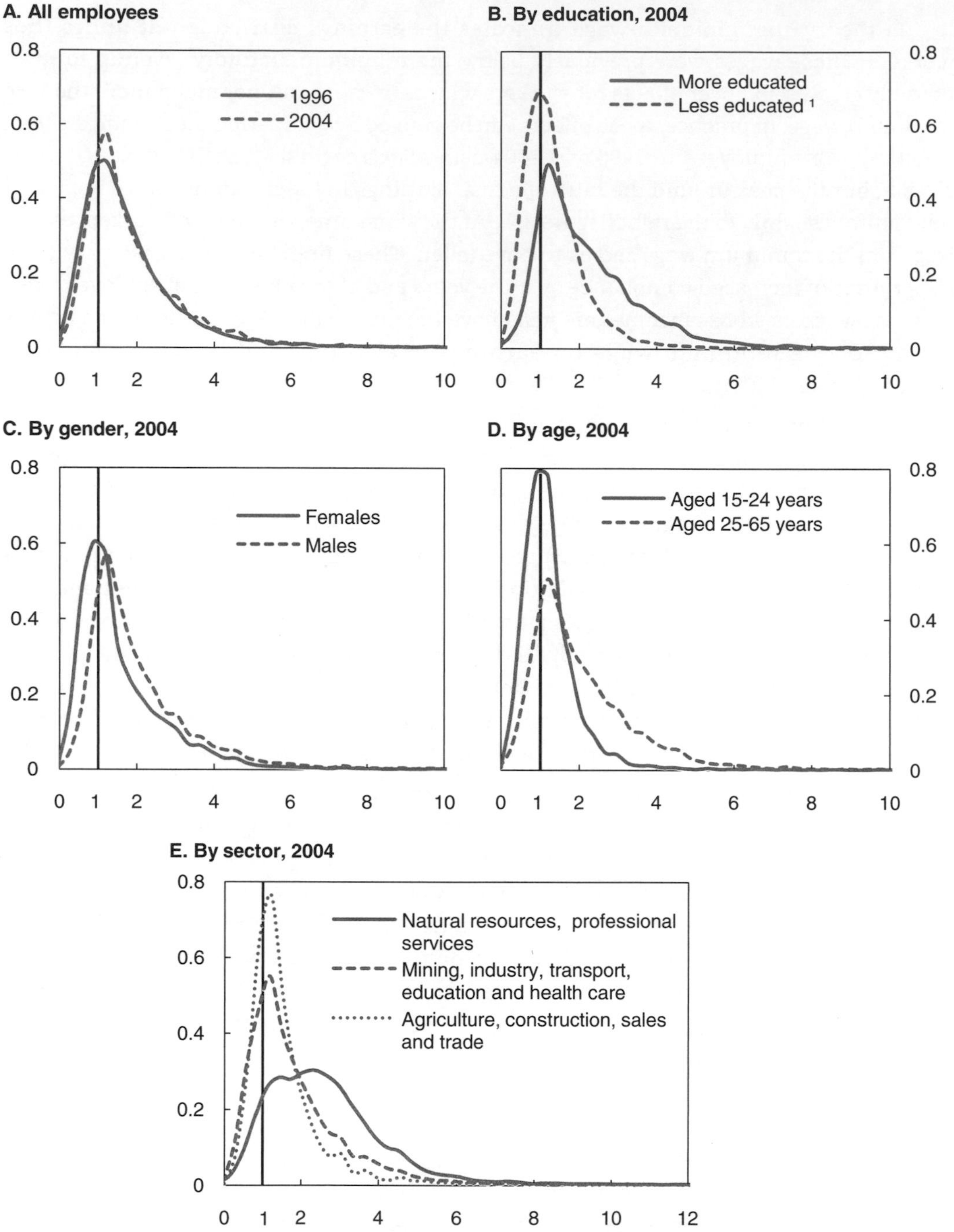

A. All employees

B. By education, 2004

C. By gender, 2004

D. By age, 2004

E. By sector, 2004

1. Employees having completed up to lower-secondary education are considered less educated.

Source: Sakernas and OECD calculations.

extent, this reflects differences in legal provisions and compliance across countries. This is the case in the OECD area too, where there are important variations in the level of the minimum wage in relation to average wages, the coverage of minimum wage provisions across sectors and age groups, the mechanisms for indexation, and the role of social partners and the government in setting the statutory minimum wage (OECD, 1998). In any case, there is fairly general agreement that the effect of the minimum wage on employment in OECD countries should be stronger, the higher its level in relation to average/median wages. It appears that individuals, such as youths, are most vulnerable to job losses due to a high minimum wage. But empirical evidence is much less conclusive for women and part-time workers (OECD, 1999).

In the case of Indonesia, there is some evidence that minimum wage legislation has had a negative effect on urban formal-sector employment. The early empirical studies tend to find only a relatively modest impact (Islam and Nazara, 2000; Rama, 2001), if at all, possibly because they focused on the period prior to the substantial increase in the real value of the minimum wage, which took place after 2000-01. More recent evidence nevertheless suggests that there may indeed be a negative employment effect, particularly for those individuals with the most precarious attachment to the labour market, such as females, youths and the less educated (Suryahadi *et al.*, 2003). This evidence is in line with the hypothesis that employers may substitute capital and skilled labour for unskilled labour as a means of mitigating the impact of increases in the real value of the minimum wage on their production costs and profit margins. This is also the experience of some countries in the OECD area (OECD, 2007a).

To shed more light on this matter, the hypothesis that minimum wage legislation, especially the sharp increase in the real value of the minimum wage before and after decentralisation in 2001, has had a bearing on unemployment was tested in Annex 3.A2. The empirical findings on the basis of local government-level data suggest that the increase in the minimum wage during 1996-2004 was associated with a rise in unemployment, controlling for other determinants of unemployment. On the basis of the estimated parameters, if the minimum wage were to be raised by 100 000 *rupiah*, for example, the unemployment rate of the population aged 15-65 would rise by 0.4 percentage points.

It should be acknowledged that, by displacing low-productivity workers, higher minimum wages may lead to productivity gains. But the extent to which this effect arises from stronger incentives for workers and employers to invest in training or from a substitution of skilled for unskilled labour is unclear. Empirical evidence is limited in this regard, even for OECD countries. In any case, the effect of minimum wage legislation on labour productivity, even if found to be strong, would need to be weighed against the welfare losses associated with lower employment opportunities for unskilled workers.

Trends in poverty and income distribution

On the basis of Indonesia's national poverty line, which is set at the provincial level for urban and rural households separately, the incidence of poverty has fallen steadily since the 1997-98 financial crisis, despite an uptick in 2006, which was essentially due to an increase in the price of rice, rather than the concomitant reduction in fuel-price subsidies. By 2004, the incidence of poverty had returned to its pre-crisis level. The poverty headcount ratio fell from a peak of just over 23% in 1999 to nearly 18% in 2006. Based on this incidence rate, nearly 40 million people still lived below the poverty line in 2006. Empirical evidence shows that an individual is most likely to be poor when he/she works in the informal sector and is poorly educated (World Bank, 2006). The incidence of poverty also varies significantly between rural and urban communities and across provinces, given Indonesia's marked disparities in living standards (discussed in Chapter 1).

Table 3.5. **Poverty and income inequality indicators, 1996 and 2005**

	1996	2005
Poverty incidence[1]		
Poverty headcount (%)	7.7	9.6
Income gap[2] (%)	15.9	19.1
Poverty gap[2] (%)	1.2	1.8
Aggregate poverty gap (million *rupiah*)	21.0	132.8
Income distribution		
Gini coefficient	0.36	0.41
Ratio of income shares of highest to lowest income deciles	4.4	5.2
Ratio of income shares of highest to lowest income quintiles	2.6	2.9
Memorandum item:		
Poverty headcount based on national poverty lines (%)	17.6	16.0

1. Based on a poverty line of one-half of median household consumption per capita (28 493 *rupiah* per capita per month in 1996 and 111 973 *rupiah* per capita per month in 2005).
2. The income gap ratio is the average per capita consumption shortfall of the population below the poverty line. It is defined as $IG = \dfrac{z - \bar{c}}{z}$, where z is the poverty line and $\bar{c}$ is average per capita consumption of the population below the poverty line. The poverty gap ratio is the sum of the income gap ratios for the population below the poverty line divided by total population. It is defined as $PG = \dfrac{1}{n}\sum_{i=1}^{q}\dfrac{(z - c_i)}{z}$, where n is total population, c_i is per capita consumption of household i and q is the population below the poverty line. Therefore, the poverty gap ratio can be calculated as the product of the income gap ratio and the headcount ratio.
3. *Source:* Susenas and OECD calculations.

An alternative measure of poverty, defined as one-half of median household consumption per capita, points to a lower incidence of poverty relative to that calculated on the basis of the national poverty line (Table 3.5). Comparison of the incidence of poverty associated with both poverty lines in 2005 shows that there is a concentration of individuals around the national poverty threshold (Figure 3.5). This is confirmed by the

Figure 3.5. **Poverty incidence, 2005**

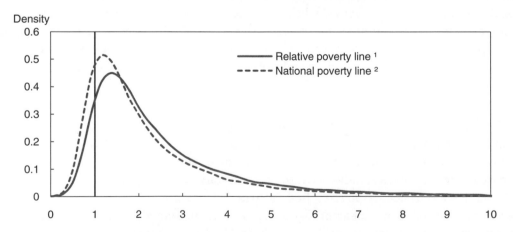

1. Defined as one-half of median household consumption per capita (111 973 *rupiah* per capita per month in 2005).
2. The BPS poverty line is the weighted average of the rural and urban poverty lines.
Source: Susenas and OECD calculations.

associated income and poverty gap ratios, which are fairly low, suggesting that the consumption level of the average poor individual is close to that implied by the national poverty line. On the basis of this alternative measure of poverty, both the headcount ratio and inequality (as gauged by the Gini coefficient and relative income shares) rose between 1996 and 2005.

The incidence of poverty has been affected by developments in the labour market. Job creation has slowed down in the formal sector since the 1997-98 financial crisis. Until then, a reduction in poverty was closely associated with a substantial shift out of agriculture and the informal sector. Poverty rates fell by close to one percentage point per year. By contrast, the reduction in poverty after the crisis has been less than one-half of a percentage point per year during 2002-07, when the official poverty rate fell from 18.2 to 16.6% of the population on the basis of the national poverty line.

Policy considerations

The overall policy message

Indonesia's labour code is rigid in relation to most comparator countries in the OECD area, and particularly against regional peers. It has also become more restrictive over time, especially after enactment of the Manpower Law of 2003. To a large extent, this trend needs to be assessed against a background of a newly enfranchised labour movement with the return to democracy after the fall of the Suharto government in 1998. It also reflects growing demands for enhanced social protection against adverse economic shocks, such as those brought about by the 1997-98 financial crisis, especially for the most vulnerable social groups. In this context, the strengthening of severance and long-service compensation rights in the case of regular contracts is understandable. So are the efforts to restore the purchasing power of the minimum wage following the rise in inflation and the job losses associated with crisis-induced output volatility over the last ten years.

Nevertheless, in an environment of already widespread labour informality, strict EPL is likely to exacerbate segmentation in the labour market, which is undesirable, instead of strengthening effective social protection for the needy, which would be welcome. It should also be recognised that a restrictive labour code secures protection for formal-sector workers, who are typically better educated and more able to fend for themselves against adverse economic shocks, to the detriment of those in the informal sector and with the most tenuous attachment to the formal labour market, such as women and youths. Therefore, to the extent that burdensome labour laws penalise vulnerable workers instead of protecting them, their use as a social protection device should be reconsidered.

Policy action could therefore focus on making labour legislation more flexible for both regular and temporary/fixed-term contracts. A review of the 2003 Manpower Law – which was planned for 2005-06 but did not come to fruition – would provide an invaluable opportunity for making progress in this important policy area. Several options are proposed below for achieving this goal, while bearing in mind the need to strengthen Indonesia's social protection programmes. The authorities' efforts to create formal safety nets since the 1997-98 crisis through community-based and targeted income transfers to vulnerable and poor individuals are commendable. Additional policy options for further improvement in this area are also discussed below.

Making the labour code more flexible

The provisions of Indonesia's EPL that are least conducive to improvements in labour-market outcomes are related to dismissal procedures, severance compensation entitlements, restrictions on flexible work arrangements and minimum-wage setting. Reform in these areas is therefore likely to yield important dividends in terms of improved labour-market performance. A few options (listed below) could be considered.

Procedures for dismissals in the case of regular contracts could be simplified. The need for recourse to a third party for approval of dismissals is not unique to Indonesia's labour code. This is also the case in a few countries in the OECD area. But the Indonesian procedures are very time-consuming, especially because of the need for the employer to send three letters to the employee to be dismissed within intervals of at least six months between letters. There is therefore considerable scope for simplifying these procedures.

The burden of severance pay on employers could be reduced. A case can be made for maintaining somewhat generous severance compensation entitlements, because unemployment insurance is not yet available in Indonesia. But there are options for making these entitlements less burdensome on employers. For example, the requirement to double the amount of severance pay that currently exists for certain types of separation, such as dismissal for economic reasons, retirement and death/invalidity, could be scrapped. Another option would be to cap the level of severance pay at a lower number of months of pay (against nine months for nine or more years of service, as in the current system).

Long-term service compensation also imposes a financial burden on employers, which could be alleviated. To achieve this goal, the cap on compensation could be reduced from the current level of 10 months for workers with at least 24 years of service. Entitlement to this compensation could also be tightened by raising the number of years of service (from currently three years) before a worker can claim long-term service pay in the event of separation. In any case, it could be argued that the burden of this entitlement could be shifted to the employee, or at least shared between employers and employees. This is because the requirement for employer-financed severance compensation already addresses the question of protecting workers against job losses in the absence of unemployment insurance. Additional protection on the grounds of length of service, if sought, could be financed privately.

Regardless of the level of severance and long-term service compensation, employers should be better prepared to deal with contingencies associated with these entitlements. There is no easy solution to this problem in a country with a still relatively thin insurance market. But a number of remedial actions can be considered. One option is to require employers to pre-finance such contingencies by depositing a share of their payroll expenses into a reserve fund. In doing so, they would accumulate a financial asset for the enterprise that could be used to finance severance-related expenses, should these contingencies materialise. Of course, a number of technical questions would need to be addressed. For example, the level of this "levy" would need to be calibrated, and prudential regulations for fund management, which could be administered privately or publicly, would need to be set, preferably by the monetary authorities.

Work arrangements could be made more flexible. Policy initiatives in this area could focus on extending the duration of temporary work, which is currently limited to three months (the probation period for regular contracts), and fixed-term contracts, which are currently limited to three years. The option of allowing an initial fixed-term contract to be drawn for three years and extended once, resulting in a maximum of six years' duration, as was the case prior to 2003, could be considered. It would also be desirable to broaden the range of activities for which fixed-term employment is permitted, beyond those of a seasonal, one-off and short-term nature. Sub-contracting could be permitted for workers performing all activities, rather than just non-core ones, provided that labour standards are maintained. These proposals are in line with those put forward by the Labour Ministry in 2006 when reviewing the 2003 Manpower Law.

Further increases in the real value of the minimum wage should be resisted. The mechanism for setting its value against benchmarks of basic consumption needs is welcome, and greater involvement of the statistics authorities in the calculation of the district-level consumption baskets and relevant price indices is a step in the direction of rendering minimum wage setting as technically sound as possible. The option envisaged by the labour code, but allegedly scarcely utilised, to allow deviations of the minimum wage from the benchmarks in periods of adverse economic conditions is also appropriate as a means of ensuring flexibility in an otherwise rigid procedure. But, at about 65% of the median wage, the minimum wage is already relatively high in Indonesia in comparison with OECD countries. At the same time, it is a poor instrument for fighting poverty, because it is not binding in the informal sector, where incomes are likely to be lower. Increases in the minimum wage are also likely to displace vulnerable workers, whose attachment to formal-sector jobs is most tenuous, in addition to pushing up prices, which tends to affect poor households more adversely than the non-poor.[7]

Therefore, the option of capping minimum wage hikes should be considered so as to alleviate the adverse impact of high minimum wages (in relation to the median) on employment, especially for low-skilled individuals, and to facilitate the formalisation of labour relations. For example, further increases in the real value of the minimum wage could be capped by increases in measured value added per worker so as to prevent increases in the real value of the minimum wages that would be out of step with productivity trends. This, or, if it were possible, a gradual reduction over time would help to alleviate the adverse employment impact of such a high minimum wage on labour-market outcomes, provided that compensatory measures could be put in place to boost social protection (discussed below).

Boosting social protection while making EPL more flexible

Restrictive labour laws have often been justified as a surrogate safety net in countries with minimal social protection programmes. Undoubtedly, there is a strong link between poverty and labour-market outcomes, given that those individuals with a precarious labour-market status are overrepresented among the poor.[8] However, a stringent labour code provides an inadequate safety net to the extent that it perpetuates segmentation in the labour market and fails to protect vulnerable workers. A policy shift would therefore be welcome: emphasis could be placed on building effective social assistance programmes while making the labour code more flexible. This policy strategy would be laudable in its own right and could help to overcome resistance to reforms, notably to the liberalisation of the labour code. In any case, enhanced social protection should seek to strengthen the incentives for workers to seek formal-sector jobs.

Once other social protection programmes have been adequately costed and implemented, unemployment insurance could be introduced over the longer term in lieu of onerous dismissal/severance compensation entitlements. The design of unemployment insurance varies significantly across countries, and several reform options are available for consideration. Nevertheless, international experience suggests that, for such a programme to be affordable and to encourage the formalisation of labour relations, it should meet a number of requirements. In particular, the duration of benefits should be limited (and possibly declining during the spell), eligibility should be conditional on a minimum duration of employment, and the programme's financial burden should be shared between employers and employees. Moreover, the need for capacity building to design and administer a cost-effective unemployment insurance, including through the enforcement of job-search requirements, should not be underestimated.

Participation in *Jamsostek* could be extended to the self-employed and to employees in smaller enterprises on an optional basis, as was recommended at the time the scheme was created in 1992. This initiative, which was taken into account in the new Social Security Law (*Jamsosnas*) enacted in 2004, would go in the direction of strengthening social insurance by broadening the array of options for saving for retirement and by facilitating access to health insurance for a larger number of workers and their families, especially those working in the informal sector. But the programme currently suffers from a lack of credibility, as evidenced by high non-compliance even among large-company employees, for whom enrolment is compulsory. Effort should therefore be put into enhancing enforcement and creditability in the programme so as to increase compliance and to encourage individuals who can afford to, but currently prefer not to participate. Of course, the attractiveness of membership depends ultimately on the perceived benefits of coverage and the affordability of contributions, which may be a significant constraint for individuals on low incomes. As a result, there is no guarantee that the workers who are currently ineligible for membership would be interested in contributing once access restrictions have been relaxed. But the exclusion of own-account workers and employees in small enterprises does impose an undue constraint on the expansion of membership.

Tackling informality, which is closely related to precariousness in the labour market and poverty, requires action in different policy areas. Informality is a multi-dimensional phenomenon, but low human capital tends to be a key determinant on the basis of the empirical evidence reported in this chapter. In most countries, informality is associated with low human capital, because the productivity of unskilled workers is too low to compensate for the costs borne by employers arising from taxation and compliance with the labour code. Efforts to boost human capital, through the educational system, labour training and skill certification, as discussed elsewhere in this *Economic Assessment*, would therefore also address this root cause of informality. The authorities are fully aware of the need to make progress in this area. In addition, policy actions that would make for a better business environment (discussed in Chapter 2), including through the removal of restrictions on business registration and of constraints to entrepreneurship in general, would also go in the same direction.

Greater conditionality could be introduced in social assistance programmes. Indonesia already has a number of formal, government-financed safety nets (Box 3.4). The newer programmes tend to be better designed and managed, and more tightly targeted than the earlier initiatives, which focused on income support to alleviate the hardships associated with economic crises, such as that of 1997-98. Emphasis is now shifting towards enhancing social assistance by equipping vulnerable individuals to pull themselves out of poverty, as in the case of *Program Keluarga Harapan*. Several programmes, such as Brazil's *Bolsa Família*,

Box 3.4. **Poverty alleviation programmes in Indonesia: An overview**

Most poverty alleviation programmes were put in place at the time of the 1997-98 financial crisis to shield vulnerable social groups from the income losses associated with a severe contraction in economic activity. A second generation of programmes was implemented more recently to protect vulnerable individuals from the rise in fuel prices and headline inflation due to the reduction in fuel subsidies in 2005.[1]

The *Rice for Poor Families* programme

Rice for Poor Families (RASKIN) is Indonesia's main income transfer programme. It was put in place during the 1997-98 crisis to alleviate poverty through the distribution of a regular ration of subsidised rice to vulnerable households. About one-third of the population benefitted from the programme at the time of the crisis. RASKIN accounts for a substantial portion of the government's development expenditures (excluding transport and distribution costs).

The programme is estimated to be relatively well targeted: nearly 85% of the subsidy accrues to households deemed needy by village leaders. RASKIN's impact on the incidence of poverty is therefore strong: it is estimated that the poverty gap would have been 20% higher in the absence of the programme. RASKIN was also used as an additional compensatory mechanism for protecting the poor against fuel price hikes in 2002-03: one-tenth of RASKIN rations were provided as compensation for an increase in administrative fuel prices.

The *Fuel Subsidy Reduction Compensation Fund* (PKPS-BBM)

In October 2005, a programme was launched to compensate poor households for a reduction in fuel subsidies. Fuel-price hikes were substantial in response to the increase in the price of oil, which put the public finances under considerable strain. The reduction in the fuel subsidies also resulted in a sharp rise in consumer-price inflation. The ensuing savings to the budget were used to finance the provision of four targeted poverty-reduction programmes through the *Fuel Subsidy Reduction Compensation Fund* (PKPS-BBM). The programmes comprised targeted transfers to poor households to finance basic health care and insurance against income losses, a School Operational Fund (BOS), financing for the development of infrastructure at the local level and unconditional cash transfers.

Unconditional cash transfers were disbursed from October 2005 through the postal service in quarterly instalments of about USD 30 per household to 15.5 million households. Programme design and implementation has been strengthened over time, including through improvements in the cadastre of beneficiaries, payment procedures and mechanisms for dealing with grievances.

Programme evaluation

Assessments of Indonesia's major targeted income transfer programmes are by and large positive.[2] Targeting deficiencies have been identified as having resulted from the need for swift implementation in times of crisis and against a background of data constraints. But other specific features of the programmes have compensated for these targeting shortcomings. For example, identification of the targeted population has been carried out with the assistance of village leaders, who command respect among the recipient population. A preference for self-targeting methods, according to which potential beneficiaries select themselves for benefits, as well as a focus on the provision of basic necessities goods, such as low-quality rice, and workfare programmes paying below-market wages, have contributed to reducing leakages. Moreover, there is little evidence to suggest that these programmes are contributing to the creation of poverty traps, which would discourage work effort.

> **Box 3.4. Poverty alleviation programmes in Indonesia: An overview** *(cont.)*
>
> **The next steps**
>
> The initial assessment of PKPS-BBM also proposed the introduction of conditionality in income transfer programmes so as to require beneficiaries to keep their children at school and to pay regular visits to health clinics. A pilot programme was put in place in 2007 in a few provinces. The programme is expected to be extended to other provinces in the near term.
>
> Other social assistance programmes are under way. For example, emphasis is being placed on targeted support for increasing health insurance coverage among poor households. The programme is expected to benefit 76.4 million individuals in 2008. Scholarships have also been introduced for students from disadvantaged backgrounds for a target population of nearly 38 million. Other initiatives include infrastructure development at the local level of government, potentially benefiting 60-70 million individuals, and facilitated access to credit for poor individuals.
>
> 1. See Asian Development Bank (2006) for more information.
> 2. See Perdana and Maxwell (2004), Sumarto *et al.* (2004) and World Bank (2006) for more information.

Chile's *Chile Solidario* and Mexico's *Progresa/Oportunidades*, show that conditionality is a key to effectively linking social protection to durable improvements in social outcomes. Eligibility requirements related to school enrolment and visits to health clinics are among the most effective requirements.

Fuel and electricity subsidies could be reduced further. As discussed in Chapter 1, based on official projections, outlays on subsidies are expected to account for nearly 20% of government expenditure in 2008. Fuel subsidies alone are projected to account for the bulk of this amount, despite the large increase in domestic prices that took place in May. Price subsidies are undesirable for a number of reasons, as discussed elsewhere in this *Economic Assessment*. Because they are on balance poorly targeted, these subsidies reduce the overall progressivity of social spending and divert scarce budgetary resources to the financing of programmes that do not reach the most vulnerable segments of society. A capping of the electricity subsidy to the level of consumption of low-income individuals could therefore be considered as a means of improving the incidence of government spending on this programme. Also, the introduction of an explicit mechanism for setting domestic prices in line with international prices would release pressure from the budget at times of surging international fuel prices. In both cases, the attendant budgetary savings could be used to increase appropriations for the better-targeted, conditional income-support programmes discussed above, as well as for human capital accumulation and infrastructure development.

An important, more fundamental policy consideration is how to finance social protection over the longer term. As Indonesia's formal safety nets are broadened and strengthened, they will exert growing pressure on the budget. The tradeoffs associated with different funding instruments will therefore become increasingly prominent in the policy debate. Most countries rely on a combination of general taxation and social contributions to finance social protection. But the impact of these different instruments on employment and welfare differs considerably, depending on the tax wedge they impose on labour income. OECD experience suggests that the negative employment effects of the tax

3. IMPROVING LABOUR MARKET OUTCOMES

wedge are especially strong for low-paid employment, notably in the presence of a binding minimum wage.

A summary of policy considerations is presented in Box 3.5.

Box 3.5. **Summary of policy considerations for improving labour-market outcomes**

Options for making the labour code more flexible

- Procedures for dismissals could be simplified in the case of regular contracts.
- The burden of severance pay could be reduced, and the cost of long-term service compensation could be shared between employees and employers.
- A mechanism could be created for employers to pre-fund contingencies associated with severance compensation entitlements.
- The maximum duration of fixed-term contracts could be extended, and the range of activities for which temporary work contracts are allowed could be broadened.
- Real increases in the minimum wage could be capped so as not to exceed labour productivity gains.

Options for boosting social protection while making EPL more flexible

- Once other social protection programmes have been adequately costed and implemented, unemployment insurance could be introduced over the longer term in lieu of onerous dismissal/severance compensation entitlements.
- Once *Jamsostek* has been strengthened and credibility in the institution has been bolstered, participation in *Jamsostek* could be extended to the self-employed and employees in smaller enterprises on an optional basis.
- Conditionality could be enhanced in social assistance programmes (*Program Keluarga Harapan*).
- Fuel and electricity subsidies could be reduced further and the associated budgetary savings could be used to finance more meritorious social programmes (social protection and human capital development) and infrastructure development (discussed in Chapters 1 and 2).

Notes

1. See Manning and Roesad (2007) for a comprehensive overview of the 2003 Manpower Law and other labour-related legislation, as well the information reported on the website of the International Labour Organisation (*www.ilo.org/public/english/dialogue/ifpdial/info/termination/ countries/indonesia.htm*).

2. The Law also requires payment of compensation for unused annual leave, transport costs to the worker's place of domicile prior to taking up employment, and, where applicable, housing allowance, and medical and health care at a rate of 15% of the standard severance and long-term service compensation.

3. Until end-2000, there were different minimum wages within a few provinces (Riau, South Sumatra, West Java, East Java and Bali), and for selected sectors of activity.

4. The 2000 law sets the conditions for the creation of trade unions and their organisational structure (*e.g.* minimum membership requirements for enterprise unions, federations and confederations). Currently, there are three major union confederations representing some 10 million workers, or around 25-30% of formal-sector workers. A plethora of smaller confederations cover about 5 million workers representing specific industries and having greater influence in certain regions,

such as East Java and North Sumatra. Less than one-half of non-agricultural salaried workers are unionised, and probably around one-half of these workers do not pay their union dues on a regular basis.

5. The industrial relations law replaced the Disputes Councils, which used to be administered by the provinces and the central government with trade union and employer representation, by civil courts for labour disputes.

6. Unfortunately, *Sakernas* does not report earnings for non-employees. This lack of information on earnings for individuals whose employment status is most likely to be correlated with informality makes it impossible to test empirically for the presence of possible spillovers from formal-sector wage setting on the informal sector. In some countries, such as Brazil, for example, there is evidence that, to different degrees, the effects of changes in the minimum wage on the earnings distribution are not limited to the formal sector.

7. The simulations reported by Bird and Manning (2005) show that about one-half of the benefits from the hike in the minimum wage in 2003 would accrue to non-poor households. Despite an increase in earnings, poor households also suffer from a minimum wage-induced rise in inflation and attendant job losses, especially among the unskilled.

8. See Alisjahbana and Manning (2006) for more discussion.

Bibliography

Alisjahbana, A.S. and C. Manning (2006), "Labour Market Dimensions of Poverty in Indonesia", *Bulletin of Indonesian Economic Studies*, Vol. 42, pp. 235-61.

Arifianto, A. (2004), "Social Security Reform in Indonesia: An Analysis of the National Social Security Bill (RUU *Jamsosnas*)", *Working Paper*, SMERU, Jakarta.

Asian Development Bank (2005), *Labour Markets in Asia: Promoting Full, Productive, and Decent Employment*, Key Indicator Series, Asian Development Bank, Manila.

Asian Development Bank (2006), *From Poverty to Prosperity: A Country Poverty Analysis for Indonesia*, Asian Development Bank, Manila.

Bird, K. and C. Manning (2005), "Minimum Wages and Poverty in a Developing Country: Simulations from Indonesia's Household Survey", unpublished manuscript, Australian National University, Camberra.

Bourguignon, F., M. Fournier and M. Gurgand (2001), "Selection Bias Correction Based on the Multinomial Logit Model", *CREST Working Paper*, 2001.

Gasparini, L. and L. Tornarolli (2007), "Labour Informality in Latin America and the Caribbean: Patterns and Trends from Household Survey Microdata", *Working Paper*, No. 0, CEDLAS, Universidad Nacional de La Plata, La Plata, Argentina.

Heckman, J. (1979), "Sample Selection Bias as a Specification Error", *Econometrica*, Vol. 47, pp. 153-61.

Hill, A. (1983), "Female Labour Force Participation in Developing and Developed Countries. Consideration on the Informal Sector", *Review of Economics and Statistics*, Vol. 65, pp. 459-68.

International Labour Organisation (2003), *Social Security and Coverage for All: Restructuring the Social Security Scheme in Indonesia – Issues and Options*, International Labour Organisation, Jakarta.

Islam, I. and S. Nazara (2000), "Minimum Wage and the Welfare of Indonesian Workers", *Occasional Discussion Paper*, No. 3, International Labour Organisation, Jakarta.

Jaffe, A.J. and K. Azumi (1960), "The Birth Rate and Cottage Industry in Underdeveloped Countries", *Economic Development and Cultural Change*, Vol. 9, pp. 52-63.

Leechor, C. (1996), "Reforming Indonesia's Pension System", *Policy Research Working Paper*, No. 1677, World Bank, Washington, D.C.

Maloney, W. (2004), "Informality Revisited", *World Development*, Vol. 32, pp. 1159-78.

Manning, C. and K. Roesad (2007), "The Manpower Law of 2003 and Its Implementing Regulations: Genesis, Key Articles and Potential Impact", *Bulletin of Indonesian Economic Studies*, Vol. 43, pp. 59-86.

OECD (1998), OECD *Employment Outlook*, OECD, Paris.

OECD (1999), OECD *Employment Outlook*, OECD, Paris.

OECD (2003), *OECD Economic Survey of Chile*, OECD, Paris.

OECD (2004a), *OECD Employment Outlook*, OECD, Paris.

OECD (2004b), *OECD Economic Survey of Brazil*, OECD, Paris.

OECD (2007a), *OECD Employment Outlook*, OECD, Paris.

OECD (2007b), *OECD Economic Survey of India*, OECD, Paris.

OECD (2008a), *Pensions at a Glance – Asia/Pacific*, OECD, Paris.

OECD (2008b), *OECDEconomic Assessment of South Africa*, OECD, Paris.

Perdana, A.A. and J. Maxwell (2004), "Poverty Targeting in Indonesia: Programs, Problems and Lessons Learned", *Economics Working Paper*, No. 83, Centre for Strategic and International Studies (CSIS), Jakarta.

Rama, M. (2001), "The Consequences of Doubling the Minimum Wage: The Case of Indonesia", *Industrial and Labour Relations Review*, Vol. 54, pp. 864-81.

Sugiyarto, G., M. Oey-Gardiner and N. Triaswati (2006), "Labour Markets in Indonesia: Key Challenges and Policy Issues", in J. Felipe and R. Hasan (eds.), *Labour Market Issues in Asia*, Asian Development Bank, Manila.

Sumarto, S., A. Suryahadi and W. Widyanti (2004), "Assessing the Impact of Indonesian Social Safety Net Programs on Household Welfare and Poverty Dynamics", *Working Paper*, SMERU, Jakarta.

Suryahadi, A., W. Widyanti, D. Perwira and S. Sumarto (2003), "Minimum Wage Policy and Its Impact on Employment in the Urban Formal Sector", *Bulletin of Indonesian Economic Studies*, Vol. 39, pp. 29-50.

World Bank (2006), *Making the NewIndonesia Work for the Poor*, World Bank, Washington, D.C.

ANNEX 3.A1

The determinants of employment and earnings

This Annex reports the estimation of employment and wage equations using data available from the National Labour Force Survey (*Sakernas*) carried out by BPS on an annual basis. *Sakernas* started to be collected in 1976 and focuses on the socio-economic and labour market characteristics of individuals and households. Two waves of *Sakernas* (1996 and 2004) are used in this empirical analysis.

Data

Data on earnings and employment are reported in *Sakernas* as follows. Each family member belonging to the working-age population (those aged 10 years and above until 1997, and 15 years and above since 1998) is classified as employed or unemployed depending on his/her activities during the previous week. Employed individuals are classified as employees (salaried workers), employers, self-employed or unpaid workers. While *Sakernas* data are considered to be good, there are two main issues that need to be dealt with in empirical analysis. *First*, earnings data are collected for employees only, thus excluding a large number of workers, including those in the informal sector. *Second*, to the extent that individuals working in the informal sector declare themselves to be employees, the true number of employees is likely to be overestimated. This is the case of agricultural workers, for example, since a non-negligible share of these workers declares themselves as employees, when in fact they are likely to work informally.

The results

Wage and employment equations

Table 3.A1.1 reports the results of the estimation of a standard OLS wage equation for 1996 and 2004 separately for a sample of individuals aged 15-65 years who have worked at least one hour as salaried workers over the previous week. The dependent variable is the logarithm of individual hourly wages.[1] The results are as expected: wages rise with educational attainment and age (albeit for age in a non-linear manner), women are paid less than men, being married is associated with a wage premium in the labour market, workers are better paid in industry than in agriculture or services, and there are important regional effects on earnings. Family background matters, given that wages rise with the average years of schooling of other household members. Moreover, comparison of the results for 1996 and 2004 is instructive. The returns to education (*i.e.* the marginal effect of education on earnings) appear to have increased for the individuals with at least tertiary education. On the other hand, the negative wage premium associated with women seems to have weakened. Some of the provincial effects also changed, possibly reflecting changes in the geographical distribution of economic activity and growth.

Although intuitive, these results are likely to suffer from a selection bias, which needs to be corrected. This is because all *Sakernas* respondents are asked their employment status (self-employed, employer, employee or unpaid worker), but information on earnings is collected only for employees, as mentioned above. Since it is unlikely that individuals sort themselves into the different employment statuses at random, a selection bias may arise if a standard Mincerian wage equation is estimated with earnings data for employees only. In fact, there may be significant differences between employees and workers with different job statuses.[2] In particular, an estimation bias occurs if selection into the different job statuses is related to unobservable covariates that help to explain the dependent variable (hourly wages).

A standard sample-selection correction technique is proposed by Heckman (1979), who defines the selection-bias problem as one arising from omitted variables. A method for correcting this bias consists of inserting the omitted variable in the form of the inverse Mills ratio (i.e. the ratio of the probability density function over the cumulative density function of a distribution) into the wage equation. We use instead a generalisation of this technique using as the selection equation the multinomial logit model proposed by Bourguignon, Fournier and Gurgand (2001). Accordingly, the set of labour force alternatives is expanded to three possibilities: working as an employee, working but not as an employee, and not working at all. The category "working but not as an employee" includes the self-employed, employers and unpaid workers, who can be considered as informal-sector workers. Therefore, this characterisation of the employment statuses is consistent with a decision tree according to which workers sort themselves between the formal and informal sectors.

Tables 3.A1.2 and 3.A1.3 report the results of the estimations of the selection equation and the wage equation corrected for multinomial selection bias, respectively. In Table 3.A1.2, the results from the selection equation are reported for the unemployed and for formal-sector workers, given that the outcome "working but not as an employee" is the reference category. The sample includes all individuals aged 15-65 years. To fulfil the exclusion restrictions, the dependency ratio and its interaction with gender (female) are not included in the selection-corrected equation. The estimation results suggest that the probability of working as an employee rises with educational attainment, an effect that was stronger in 2004 than in 1996. Age, marital status and household educational attainment are additional powerful predictors of an individual's employment status. Living in rural areas strongly reduces the probabilities of working in the formal sector and of being unemployed. As in the wage equations, regional effects are also strong and changed in some cases during 1996-2004. In particular, these results suggest that better educated, married and older (in a non-linear manner) individuals are more likely to work in the formal sector than in the informal sector and to be unemployed.

Table 3.A1.3 reports the results of the estimation of the selection-corrected wage equation. Comparison of the results reported in Tables 3.A1.1 and 3.A1.3 reveals important differences. For example, once the selection bias has been corrected, the effect of living in rural areas on earnings becomes negative, which is more intuitive on the basis of the lower incidence of poverty in urban areas. Likewise, the effects of attending school and the interaction term *female*married* also turn negative, as expected. This evidence strongly supports the hypothesis of a selection bias in the wage equations: since rural individuals, students and married females are less likely to work as employees, it is necessary to correct for the selection bias arising from the presence of these individuals in the sample in order to obtain consistent estimates of the determinants of earnings on the basis of a survey that only reports earnings for salaried workers.

Notes

1. Respondents are asked the number of hours worked during the previous week and their average monthly wage as employees. For those employees who are temporarily out of work at the time the survey is conducted, the number of hours worked in the previous week is computed as the mean of the sample distribution.

2. In developing economies it is common practice to consider self-employed and family workers as working in the informal sector and employees as working in the formal sector (Jaffe and Azumi, 960; Hill, 1983). However, this may not be true in our sample, because individuals working independently in the informal sector may define themselves as employees. Therefore, the true number of employees reported may be overestimated in *Sakernas*.

Table 3.A1.1. **Wage equations, 1996 and 2004**[1]

(Dep. Var.: Logarithm of hourly wage)

	1996	2004
Rural	0.0216***	0.002
	(0.002)	(0.79)
Female	−0.303***	−0.214***
	(0.000)	(0.000)
Age	0.0379***	0.0395***
	(0.000)	(0.000)
Age_squared	−0.000323***	−0.000309***
	(0.000)	(0.000)
Married	0.137***	0.0954***
	(0.000)	(0.000)
Female*married	0.0757***	0.0328**
	(0.000)	(0.01)
Attending_school	0.049	0.0749**
	(0.14)	(0.014)
Schooling_primary	0.141***	0.129***
	(0.000)	(0.000)
Schooling_low_secondary	0.322***	0.329***
	(0.000)	(0.000)
Schooling_upp_secondary	0.643***	0.640***
	(0.000)	(0.000)
Schooling_tertiary	1.068***	1.133***
	(0.000)	(0.000)
Average_adult_schooling	0.00794***	0.0133***
	(0.000)	(0.000)
Province 12	−0.0793***	−0.034
	(0.003)	(0.27)
Province 13	−0.121***	−0.058
	(0.000)	(0.13)
Province 14	0.041	0.165***
	(0.17)	(0.000)
Province 15	−0.043	−0.028
	(0.17)	(0.54)
Province 16	−0.039	−0.044
	(0.18)	(0.24)
Province 17	−0.139***	−0.197***
	(0.000)	(0.000)
Province 18	−0.314***	−0.164***
	(0.000)	(0.000)
Province 19		0.182***
		(0.000)
Province 31	0.0924***	0.111***
	(0.000)	(0.000)
Province 32	−0.0699***	−0.0636**
	(0.003)	(0.033)
Province 33	−0.291***	−0.256***
	(0.000)	(0.000)
Province 34	−0.320***	−0.308***
	(0.000)	(0.000)
Province 35	−0.296***	−0.200***
	(0.000)	(0.000)
Province 36		0.107***
		(0.001)
Province 51	−0.143***	−0.012
	(0.000)	(0.71)

Table 3.A1.1. **Wage equations, 1996 and 2004**[1] (cont.)

(Dep. Var.: Logarithm of hourly wage)

	1996	2004
Province 52	−0.288***	−0.317***
	(0.000)	(0.000)
Province 53	−0.363***	−0.100**
	(0.000)	(0.016)
Province 61	0.024	0.04
	(0.44)	(0.25)
Province 62	0.008	0.198***
	(0.82)	(0.000)
Province 63	−0.041	0.0663*
	(0.18)	(0.058)
Province 64	0.119***	0.144***
	(0.000)	(0.000)
Province 71	−0.249***	0.0934**
	(0.000)	(0.011)
Province 72	−0.334***	−0.048
	(0.000)	(0.29)
Province 73	−0.178***	−0.016
	(0.000)	(0.68)
Province 74	−0.112***	−0.101**
	(0.001)	(0.046)
Province 75		−0.136**
		(0.01)
Province 81	−0.0893***	0.0864**
	(0.008)	(0.04)
Province 82	0.258***	0.235***
	(0.000)	(0.001)
Province 94	0.228***	0.474***
	(0.000)	(0.000)
Sector: Agriculture-mining	−0.141***	0.107***
	(0.000)	(0.000)
Sector: Industry	0.0174**	0.229***
	(0.029)	(0.000)
Sector: Trade-services	−0.0576***	0.0930***
	(0.000)	(0.000)
Constant	5.629***	6.566***
	(0.000)	(0.000)
No. of observations	45 241	38 505

1. All models are estimated by OLS. Statistical significance at the 1%, 5% and 10% levels is denoted by (***), (**) and (*), respectively. Heteroscedasticity-corrected standard errors are reported in parentheses.
Source: Sakernas and OECD estimations.

Table 3.A1.2. **Multinomial selection employment equations, 1996 and 2004[1]**

(Dep. Var.: Not working or working as an employee)

	1996		2004	
	Not working	Working as an employee	Not working	Working as an employee
Rural	−0.1297 ***	−0.0833 ***	−0.1102 ***	−0.0954 ***
	(0.003)	(0.002)	(0.003)	(0.002)
Female	0.0928 ***	−0.0052	0.1208 ***	0.0467 ***
	(0.005)	(0.004)	(0.005)	(0.004)
Age	−0.0487 ***	0.0174 ***	−0.0561 ***	0.0147 ***
	(0.001)	(0.001)	(0.001)	(0.001)
Age_squared	0.0006 ***	−0.0003 ***	0.0007 ***	−0.0002 ***
	(0.000)	(0.000)	(0.000)	(0.000)
Married	−0.3599 ***	0.1092 ***	−0.3713 ***	0.0972 ***
	(0.006)	(0.003)	(0.006)	(0.003)
Dependency_ratio 15_65	−0.0866 ***	0.0244 ***	−0.1201 ***	0.0179 ***
	(0.006)	(0.003)	(0.010)	(0.005)
Female*married	0.5402 ***	−0.2567 ***	0.5616 ***	−0.2348 ***
	(0.005)	(0.003)	(0.005)	(0.003)
Female*dependency_ratio 15_65	0.1231 ***	−0.0472 ***	0.1596 ***	−0.0813 ***
	(0.006)	(0.004)	(0.011)	(0.007)
Attending_school	0.5174 ***	−0.2380 ***	0.5524 ***	−0.1761 ***
	(0.005)	(0.002)	(0.005)	(0.002)
Schooling_primary	−0.0384 ***	−0.0099 ***	−0.0568 ***	0.0148 ***
	(0.004)	(0.004)	(0.005)	(0.005)
Schooling_low_secondary	−0.0117 **	0.0189 ***	−0.0292 ***	0.0341 ***
	(0.006)	(0.005)	(0.006)	(0.006)
Schooling_upp_secondary	−0.0159 **	0.1685 ***	−0.0083	0.1464 ***
	(0.006)	(0.007)	(0.008)	(0.008)
Schooling_tertiary	−0.1173 ***	0.4332 ***	−0.1572 ***	0.4354 ***
	(0.008)	(0.011)	(0.008)	(0.012)
Average_adult_schooling	0.0145 ***	0.0046 ***	0.0128 ***	0.0094 ***
	(0.001)	(0.001)	(0.001)	(0.001)
Province 12	−0.0791 ***	0.1102 ***	−0.1018 ***	0.0640 ***
	(0.008)	(0.011)	(0.009)	(0.010)
Province 13	−0.0382 ***	0.0745 ***	−0.0274 **	0.0097
	(0.010)	(0.012)	(0.012)	(0.010)
Province 14	0.0522 ***	0.0496 ***	0.0744 ***	0.0434 ***
	(0.012)	(0.011)	(0.014)	(0.011)
Province 15	−0.0043	0.0457 ***	−0.0736 ***	0.0089
	(0.012)	(0.013)	(0.013)	(0.012)
Province 16	−0.0265 ***	0.0531 ***	−0.1032 ***	−0.0148
	(0.010)	(0.011)	(0.010)	(0.009)
Province 17	−0.1236 ***	0.0118	−0.1411 ***	−0.0159
	(0.010)	(0.012)	(0.011)	(0.011)
Province 18	−0.0430 ***	0.0638 ***	−0.0643 ***	−0.0167 *
	(0.010)	(0.011)	(0.011)	(0.009)
Province 19			−0.0318 **	0.1642 ***
			(0.015)	(0.017)
Province 31	0.0148	0.1437 ***	0.0170 *	0.1137 ***
	(0.010)	(0.011)	(0.010)	(0.009)
Province 32	0.0835 ***	0.1339 ***	0.0674 ***	0.0636 ***
	(0.009)	(0.009)	(0.011)	(0.009)
Province 33	−0.0915 ***	0.2084 ***	−0.1133 ***	0.0823 ***
	(0.007)	(0.011)	(0.009)	(0.010)
Province 34	−0.1488 ***	0.1344 ***	−0.1948 ***	0.0762 ***
	(0.007)	(0.012)	(0.008)	(0.012)

Table 3.A1.2. **Multinomial selection employment equations, 1996 and 2004**[1] (cont.)

(Dep. Var.: Not working or working as an employee)

	1996		2004	
	Not working	Working as an employee	Not working	Working as an employee
Province 35	−0.0537 ***	0.1810 ***	−0.0737 ***	0.0773 ***
	(0.008)	(0.010)	(0.009)	(0.009)
Province 36			0.0468 ***	0.1050 ***
			(0.013)	(0.012)
Province 51	−0.1791 ***	0.1519 ***	−0.2173 ***	0.1245 ***
	(0.007)	(0.013)	(0.007)	(0.013)
Province 52	−0.0820 ***	0.0786 ***	−0.1212 ***	−0.0206 **
	(0.009)	(0.012)	(0.010)	(0.009)
Province 53	−0.1001 ***	0.0061	−0.1635 ***	−0.0164 *
	(0.009)	(0.010)	(0.009)	(0.010)
Province 61	−0.0395 ***	0.0446 ***	−0.1091 ***	0.0869 ***
	(0.010)	(0.011)	(0.010)	(0.012)
Province 62	−0.0971 ***	−0.0159	−0.0924 ***	−0.0350 ***
	(0.010)	(0.011)	(0.012)	(0.010)
Province 63	−0.0717 ***	0.0337 ***	−0.1392 ***	0.0962 ***
	(0.010)	(0.011)	(0.010)	(0.013)
Province 64	0.0006	0.0830 ***	0.0275 *	0.0908 ***
	(0.012)	(0.013)	(0.015)	(0.014)
Province 71	0.0801 ***	0.0267 **	0.0377 **	0.0259 **
	(0.013)	(0.012)	(0.015)	(0.012)
Province 72	−0.0198 *	0.0019	−0.0730 ***	0.0149
	(0.012)	(0.011)	(0.013)	(0.012)
Province 73	0.0853 ***	−0.0227 **	0.0452 ***	−0.0120
	(0.011)	(0.009)	(0.012)	(0.009)
Province 74	−0.0602 ***	0.0287 **	−0.1120 ***	−0.0228 **
	(0.011)	(0.012)	(0.012)	(0.010)
Province 75			0.1164 ***	0.0119
			(0.018)	(0.014)
Province 81	−0.0036	0.0182	0.0069	−0.0119
	(0.012)	(0.012)	(0.016)	(0.012)
Province 82	−0.0648 ***	0.0191	−0.0705 ***	−0.0367 ***
	(0.012)	(0.013)	(0.017)	(0.013)
Province 94	0.0196	−0.0084	−0.1186 ***	−0.0045
	(0.015)	(0.013)	(0.013)	(0.013)
No. of observations	200 272	200 272	198 613	198 613

1. The models are estimated by multinomial logit, and the marginal effects are reported. Statistical significance at the 1%, 5% and 10% levels is denoted by (***), (**) and (*), respectively. Heteroscedasticity-corrected standard errors are reported in parentheses.

Source: Sakernas and OECD estimations.

Table 3.A1.3. **Selection-corrected wage equations, 1996 and 2004**[1]

(Dep. Var.: Logarithm of hourly wages)

	1996	2004
Rural	−0.127***	−0.218***
	(0.000)	(0.000)
Female	−0.291***	−0.147***
	(0.000)	(0.000)
Age	0.0437***	0.0514***
	(0.000)	(0.000)
Age_squared	−0.000470***	−0.000563***
	(0.000)	(0.000)
Married	0.187***	0.144***
	(0.000)	(0.000)
Female*married	−0.117***	−0.291***
	(0.000)	(0.000)
Attending_school	−0.021	−0.337***
	(0.65)	(0.000)
Schooling_primary	0.0957***	0.116***
	(0.000)	(0.000)
Schooling_low_secondary	0.317***	0.357***
	(0.000)	(0.000)
Schooling_upp_secondary	0.820***	0.880***
	(0.000)	(0.000)
Schooling_tertiary	1.450***	1.623***
	(0.000)	(0.000)
Average_adult_schooling	0.0186***	0.0323***
	(0.000)	(0.000)
Province 12	−0.006	0.0447*
	(0.8)	(0.086)
Province 13	−0.0500*	−0.049
	(0.068)	(0.1)
Province 14	0.0936***	0.267***
	(0.001)	(0.000)
Province 15	−0.005	−0.019
	(0.86)	(0.59)
Province 16	−0.023	−0.106***
	(0.38)	(0.001)
Province 17	−0.178***	−0.237***
	(0.000)	(0.000)
Province 18	−0.299***	−0.207***
	(0.000)	(0.000)
Province 19		0.403***
		(0.000)
Province 31	0.227***	0.302***
	(0.000)	(0.000)
Province 32	0.0751***	0.0627**
	(0.003)	(0.012)
Province 33	−0.147***	−0.158***
	(0.000)	(0.000)
Province 34	−0.267***	−0.235***
	(0.000)	(0.000)
Province 35	−0.166***	−0.0933***
	(0.000)	(0.000)
Province 36		0.291***
		(0.000)
Province 51	−0.0596**	0.121***
	(0.024)	(0.000)

Table 3.A1.3. **Selection-corrected wage equations, 1996 and 2004**[1] (cont.)

(Dep. Var.: Logarithm of hourly wages)

	1996	2004
Province 52	−0.265***	−0.391***
	(0.000)	(0.000)
Province 53	−0.399***	−0.155***
	(0.000)	(0.000)
Province 61	0.0586**	0.142***
	(0.028)	(0.000)
Province 62	−0.04	0.141***
	(0.22)	(0.000)
Province 63	−0.034	0.178***
	(0.22)	(0.000)
Province 64	0.193***	0.298***
	(0.000)	(0.000)
Province 71	−0.220***	0.140***
	(0.000)	(0.000)
Province 72	−0.355***	−0.051
	(0.000)	(0.15)
Province 73	−0.205***	−0.027
	(0.000)	(0.35)
Province 74	−0.126***	−0.184***
	(0.000)	(0.000)
Province 75		−0.0791*
		(0.056)
Province 81	−0.0905***	0.056
	(0.003)	(0.15)
Province 82	0.261***	0.115**
	(0.000)	(0.026)
Province 94	0.254***	0.443***
	(0.000)	(0.000)
Sector: Agriculture-mining	−0.145***	0.0989***
	(0.000)	(0.000)
Sector: Industry	0.0179**	0.222***
	(0.02)	(0.000)
Sector: Trade-services	−0.0535***	0.0857***
	(0.000)	(0.000)
_m0	−0.520***	−0.204***
	(0.000)	(0.000)
_m1	0.0715**	0.389***
	(0.013)	(0.000)
_m2	−1.149***	−0.810***
	(0.000)	(0.000)
Constant	4.730***	5.363***
	(0.000)	(0.000)
No. of observations	45 241	38 505

1. Statistical significance at the 1%, 5% and 10% levels is denoted by (***), (**) and (*), respectively. Heteroscedasticity-corrected standard errors are reported in parentheses.
Source: Sakernas and OECD estimations.

ANNEX 3.A2

The impact of minimum wage legislation on unemployment

This Annex tests the hypothesis that minimum wage legislation affects unemployment in Indonesia using data from two rounds of *Sakernas*, 1996 and 2004, one before and one after the devolution of responsibility over minimum-wage setting to the local governments and the sharp increase in the real value of the minimum wage in 2000-01. As opposed to the analysis reported in Annex 3.A1, emphasis is now placed on local government-level, instead of individual-level, data.

The methodology

The dependent variable used in the reduced-form unemployment regressions is defined as change in the unemployment rate of individuals aged 15-65 during 1996-2004. The independent variable of interest is the change in the nominal value of the minimum wage (in millions of *rupiah*) during 1996-2004. Additional variables are also included in the regressions to control for initial conditions, such as the unemployment rate, the shares of population with no schooling and having attained upper-secondary education, the rate of labour force participation, all computed for population aged 15-65 and for 1996. Also the employment shares by sector (agriculture and industry) in 1996, and total industrial value added in 1997 (in ten trillions of *rupiah*) are included among the controls. Data are available from *Sakernas* and *Statistik Industri* (in the case of industrial value added). The sample includes 262 local governments with complete data for both 1996 and 2004.*

The findings

The regressions were estimated by weighted OLS, where the weights are inversely proportional to the variance of district population in 1996. The results, reported in Table 3.A2.1, show that the increase in the minimum wage over the period of analysis by about 100 000 *rupiah* in nominal terms was associated with a rise in unemployment by 0.4 percentage points. There is no evidence that this association is driven by a possible

---

* Indonesia also underwent a major administrative restructuring during the period of analysis. The procedure for coding district-level data therefore involved some judgment. For the several districts that were split between 1996 and 2004, the newly-formed districts were labelled under the original name. Whenever two jurisdictions had the same name in 1996, as in the case of *kabupaten* and *kota* with the same name, they were merged in one single jurisdiction for simplicity. All variables of interest were subsequently averaged (weighted by population) for each district.

endogeneity bias: changes in the minimum wage were found to be exogenous on the basis of the Durbin-Wu-Hausman test.

The controls are signed by and large as expected: unemployment tends to have increased less in districts with a better educated labour force and with higher informality, proxied by the share of resident population engaged in agricultural activities, which is likely to absorb displaced formal-sector workers. Also, the rise in unemployment tends to be less severe in districts with a higher share of resident population employed in industry. Finally, unemployment rose faster in the larger districts, where value added is concentrated.

Although they do not seem to suffer from an endogeneity bias, these findings should be interpreted with some caution. The estimations were carried out for district-level data, which raises econometric issues related to identification and potential selection biases, which can only be appropriately addressed using individual-level data.

Table 3.A2.1. **Effect of minimum wage of unemployment, 1996-2004**[1]

(Dep. Var.: Change in unemployment during 1996-2004)

Regressors	Coefficients
Change in the value of the minimum wage (1996-2004)	0.04 **
	(0.021)
Unemployment (1996)	−0.79 ***
	(0.077)
Share of population with no schooling (1996)	−0.06 ***
	(0.019)
Share of population with upper-secondary education (1996)	−0.14 ***
	(0.036)
Share of population working in agriculture (1996)	−0.09 ***
	(0.017)
Share of population working in industry (1996)	−0.06 *
	(0.034)
Labour force participation rate (1996)	−0.10 ***
	(0.033)
Industrial value added (1997)	0.05 ***
	(0.013)
Intercept	0.19 ***
	(0.024)
R-squared	0.3975
Number of observations	250

1. Statistical significance at the 1%, 5% and 10% levels is denoted by (***), (**) and (*), respectively. Heteroscedasticity-corrected standard errors are reported in parentheses.
Source: Sakernas, Statistik Industri and OECD estimations.

ISBN 978-92-64-04805-8
OECD Economic Surveys: Indonesia: Economic Assesment
© OECD 2008

List of acronyms

AFTA	ASEAN Free Trade Agreement
ASEAN	Association of Southeast Asian Nations
BI	Bank Indonesia
	Bank Sentral Republik Indonesia
BKPM	Investment Co-ordinating Board
	Badan Koordinasi Penanaman Modal
BPS	Statistics Indonesia
	Badan Pusat Statistik
DAU	General Allocation Grant
	Dana Alokasi Umum
DAK	Special Allocation Grant
	Dana Alokasi Khusus
Jamsostek	State Social Insurance Fund
	Jaminan Sosial Tenaga Kerja
KKPPI	National Committee on Policy for Accelerating Infrastructure Provision
	Komite Kebijakan Percepatan Penyediaan Infrastruktur
KPTPK	Commission for Eradication of Corruption
	Komisi Pemberantasan Tindak Pidana Korupsi
LPEM-FEUI	Institute for Economic and Social Research, Faculty of Economics, University of Indonesia
	Lembaga Penyelidikan Ekonomi dan Masyarakat, Fakultas Ekonomi, Universitas Indonesia
PLN	State electricity company
PPTAK	Financial Transactions and Analysis Centre
	Pusat Pelaporan dan Analisa Transaksi Keuangan
Sakernas	National Labour Force Survey
	Survei Tenaga Kerja Nasional
Susenas	National Socioeconomic Survey
	Survei Sosial Ekonomi Nasional
Statistik Industri	Large and Medium-Size Manufacturing Survey
	Statistik Industri

OECD PUBLICATIONS, 2, rue André-Pascal, 75775 PARIS CEDEX 16
PRINTED IN FRANCE
(10 2008 17 1 P) ISBN 978-92-64-04805-8 – No. 56265 2008